iPad

FOR PHOTOGRAPHERS

iPad

FOR PHOTOGRAPHERS

A guide to managing, editing, & displaying
photographs using your iPad

Ben Harvell & Rachael D'Cruze

ILEX

First published in the UK in 2012 by
I L E X
210 High Street
Lewes
East Sussex BN7 2NS
www.ilex-press.com

Distributed worldwide (except North America)
by Thames & Hudson Ltd., 181A High Holborn, London WC1V 7QX,
United Kingdom

Second edition revised in 2013
Copyright © 2013 The Ilex Press Limited

Publisher: Alastair Campbell
Associate Publisher: Adam Juniper
Managing Editor: Natalia Price-Cabrera
Specialist Editor: Frank Gallaugher
Editor: Tara Gallagher
Editorial Assistant: Rachel Silverlight
Creative Director: James Hollywell
Senior Designer: Ginny Zeal
Colour Origination: Ivy Press Reprographics

British Library Cataloguing-in-Publication Data
A catalogue record for this book is available from
the British Library.

ISBN: 978-1-78157-991-6

Printed and bound in China

10 9 8 7 6 5 4 3 2 1

:CONTENTS

INTRODUCTION

Photographers were always going to make a beeline for the iPad. It was inevitable. With its lustrous screen and portability, it was the obvious replacement for outdated and weighty traditional portfolios. The attraction doesn't stop at jaw-dropping looks and perfect proportions though—the iPad is much more than a glorified digital photo frame. In fact, the iPad is a constantly developing platform, and through the apps available in the App Store, is far more than even that, as this book will show you.

The iPad will serve you well as a virtual assistant, a portable editing suite, social media hub and a high-end previewing tool and storage facility. When you consider how many functions the iPad can serve, it suddenly seems rather affordable. These pages aim to equip you with the knowledge you need to utilize all the opportunities your iPad makes available and in turn will save you time and money, as well as making your workflow more enjoyable.

The Ultimate Accessory

Viewing photos on the iPad is simply a magical experience—the ability to simply reach out, touch a photograph, move it around and smoothly zoom in and out of it gives a level of interaction that has simply changed how we look at images. While the principles behind a great shot will never change, new technology has undoubtedly changed the way we take, develop, edit, and of course view our images. The speed in which we take, process, edit, and share our images is truly staggering, with social networking now an import part of how photographers work, high speed internet connections pretty much everywhere, and more advanced software all contributing. The iPad is an important part of this and has quickly established itself as the ultimate accessory for

the modern photographer. This book aims to show you just how useful the iPad is and we've even drafted in a gaggle of top professional photographers who show you how their iPads have improved their work.

All Bases Covered

Working as a freelance journalist and photographer for a range of newsstand magazines means that I, along with Ben Harvell who wrote the first edition of *iPad For Photographers*, have always had a vested professional interest in how the iPad can improve a creative working life. I simply couldn't be without one now—mine wakes me up in the morning, organizes my day alerting me to meetings and deadlines and, when I'm out of my office, I use it for writing copy, editing photographs, and sharing behind-the-scenes pictures of any interesting magazine shoots I'm on. This book will show you everything from the basics of getting photos from your DSLR onto your iPad through to editing techniques and exploring applications that will improve your workflow. We'll also explore Apple's iCloud service, which is great for photographers who wish to both secure and share their data, as well as more sharing options and mobile internet uses.

Highly Recommended

iPad for Photographers recommends a range of apps within its pages—rest assured that these are they very best available on the market today and those that are paid-for apps won't break the bank and are worth the investment, providing your iPad with far more options than it has in its default form. It's worth noting, in case you're new to apps, that once you've bought one, you'll get regular free updates

ABOVE The range of photography apps constantly being released through the iTunes App Store means that the iPad is always evolving.

RIGHT From sharing quick, behind-the-scenes shots to editing Raw images, iPad for Photographers has it covered.

so you can expect to see new features as you use them in your daily workflow.

As well as recommending a variety of apps, there's also a dedicated section for essential accessories for iPad users. Be sure to take a look, all the products we've selected will either add additional features or improve your workflow and day-to-day usage. You'll almost certainly want to invest in a case, whether you want something flashy to impress your clients or a military standard case to shield your device from the elements—after you'll want to protect your most valuable photographic accessory.

1 THE BASICS

Just like a computer, at the core of the iPad is an operating system—underlying software that drives it, allowing other features and apps to work. The operating system is absolutely critical and without it the iPad wouldn't work—a lot like the image sensor in your DSLR. The operating system provides the screens that let you switch between apps, but just as crucially it provides the tools apps need to access features of the iPad.

Apple regularly updates the software for operating systems and, usually, older systems can take advantage of many of the new features.

For example, the latest operating system update, iOS 6, includes the full set of features provided by Siri, Apple's own Maps app, seamless Facebook integration, and Sharing multiple PhotoStreams.

If you're used to updating your camera software, this might all seem like old news—but you'd be surprised at how many people never update any software and end up missing out. Don't make the mistake of activating your iPad then never connecting it to your computer again—you'll miss out on free new features and security updates.

"The operating system is absolutely critical and without it the iPad wouldn't work"

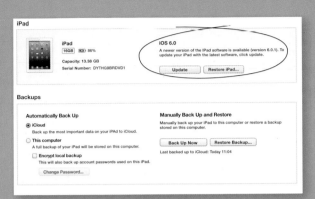

ABOVE Plug your iPad into your computer and you'll see if a newer version of iPad software is available.

ABOVE Once you've clicked "Update," you'll see a screen that tells you what benefits you are getting from updating your iPad software—you simply read and click "Next."

iOS updates

If you're not sure what version of iOS you have, plug your iPad into your computer, then click "Summary" on your iPad screen, which iTunes will automatically load. Here you'll see which version of iOS you're running and you'll be given the option of updating to iOS 6 if you haven't got it yet—which you should do, as it's brilliant! The only devise that doesn't support an upgrade to iOS 6 is the first generation iPad. For the purposes of this book you'll ideally be running iOS 6, but if not iOS 5.

Reach for the skies

iCloud is Apple's innovative storage solution that not only stores your content but lets you access your music, photos, calendars, contacts, documents from whatever device you're on: your phone, iPod, computer, or, of course, your iPad.

To use iCloud, Mac users need to make sure you are running OS X 10.7.4 or later. If you don't have the latest version of OS X installed, you can purchase it directly from the Mac App Store. PC users need to have Windows Vista with Service Pack 2 or Windows 7 installed on their PC, need to download and install the iCloud Control Panel for Windows, available at www.apple.com/uk/icloud.

Like all network-based services, you'll need an account and a password before you can get going. Once you've set that up on your computer, iPad and iPhone, if you have one, you'll find it all works together seamlessly and will make your life so much easier.

The Photo Stream feature, which is part of iCloud, is particularly useful. You'll be pleased to know it is not limited to the iPad's built-in camera, so you'll be able to transmit images from any app that uses the iPad's, or iPhone's Photo cataloging functions. Straight out of the box that includes the Photo Booth tool, but other great photo apps are also included.

ABOVE After you've connected your iPad for the first time and updated your software, iTunes will start to automatically check for updates for you.

⋮SETTING UP

On the last few pages, we talked about some of the new technologies that the iPad puts into your hands. Now we'll have a look at what you need to do to get going. We'll start right from the beginning, as if you'd just acquired a shiny new iPad, but if you've already completed some of these steps, then skim through the text and jump in where you need to.

This is my first ever Apple device, and I've never used iTunes

Really? Well, welcome to the party, as they say. Actually you've got something of an advantage, as you'll only need to set up one account, you won't need to "migrate" any information from other accounts. You will be guided through the process, and can choose either to associate it with an email account you already have, or to take advantage of Apple's free email service (with an @me.com address). It's probably better to use your normal email address though, as your Apple ID will be associated with your credit card (or debit card) too, so you can make purchases.

ABOVE & RIGHT When you switch on your iPad for the first time, you'll be invited to select your language, where you live, then—if you do not already have one—the option to create an Apple ID. An Apple ID is a single account you can use across your devices (including iTunes on a PC or a Mac).

I already use iTunes to buy music or apps

This might mean you've got an iPhone or iPod and use that to buy apps and music, or it might just mean your favorite online record store is iTunes for Windows. In any case, it means you've already got an Apple ID, so for the sake of convenience it would make sense to use that one. After all, the point of all the lovely cloudy connectivity is that we're sharing data between our devices.

You'll find your Apple ID at the top right of the window in iTunes, so you can copy this into your iPad and (if you've forgotten your password since setting the account up) there's an amusingly named "iForgot" tool to put things right.

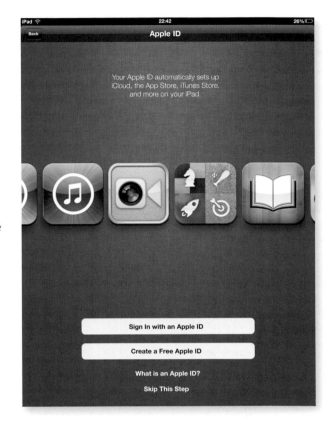

RIGHT If you already use iTunes, your Apple ID is shown here in the top left of the display area when you're browsing the iTunes Store.

:SETTING UP

Cloud services back home

Once you've got an Apple ID, you're ready to buy, but there's more to it than that. The Apple ID is also your link to iCloud services, and they work a whole lot better if your computer knows where to look.

RIGHT Creating an account with the iCloud service will allow you to use your iPad to its maximum potential.

iCloud

On a Mac

1 In Mac OS X Lion or later (10.7+), open the System Preferences panel via the Apple symbol in the top left corner of your screen, and under the Internet & Wireless header, choose iCloud.

2 Here you can connect your Apple ID to your iCloud account, and further, then sync up various other services to your iCloud.

3 Whether you want to sync up all your contacts, notes, and so on is your personal choice, but I particularly recommend activating your Photo Stream, which will automatically push your photos to all your other synced devices.

On a PC

1 If you use Windows, you'll first need to go to www.apple.com/icloud and download the iCloud for Windows tool.

2 Follow the on-screen instructions and either sign in with your Apple ID or create a new one. Then, when you see the settings screen, ensure that the Photo Stream button is checked (switched on).

3 This creates two folders in the location of your choice (by default the Pictures folder), one which receives pictures from your iPad, and the other which sends them to it.

2 IMPORTING PHOTOS

Let's face it—the iPad would be a nigh-on useless tool for the photographer without a way to add photos to the devise. Obviously, the built-in camera is one method and even though the 5MP cameras in the third and fourth generation iPads and the iPad mini are a vast improvement on the 0.7MP camera we saw in the iPad 2, they are still of camera phone quality. Great for quick behind the scenes shots for social media and the like but not for anything high quality. It's a relief to know, then, that there are several ways in which your images from your cameras can be transferred to the iPad and accessed, either by way of the built-in Photos app or through third-party photo applications. Methods include Wi-Fi and USB connections from your computer to iPad or a dedicated iPad card reader that takes both SD and CF cards, to cut out the need to use your computer. If you're planning to use the iPad as a review or editing tool it makes sense to hold

"there are several ways in which your images from your cameras can be transferred to the iPad"

of a card reader from the offset—you'll find you need to take your laptop out in the field, or on trips, very rarely.

Before you leap in transferring your photos to the iPad, you need to consider how much storage capacity you have. If you've opted for a 16GB and plan on copying over RAW files or even large-format JPEGs you will find your iPad fills up pretty quickly. If you haven't yet purchased your iPad, go for a 32GB or 64GB model.

The Settings app on the iPad home screen will show you will show you how much space you have available. This view lists all of the media present on your devise and also gives a reading of the capacity and available capacity for the drive—very handy indeed. Over the page you'll find a tutorial, which shows you exactly how to do this.

As soon as you've checked your capacity you'll notice your iPad didn't quite have the space detailed by Apple to begin with. The 16, 32 or 64GB capacity listed for iPad models doesn't include the system software or pre-installed apps that your iPad comes with, and needs to work properly, so you never actually have access to the full amount. So, the best idea is to forget about the claimed storage capacity and focus instead on real information you access on your iPad, or you'll likely end up with annoying error messages explaining that not all of your images could be transferred.

Another way to view the available space on your iPad is to connect it to your computer, via USB. Once connected, you can access the iPad through iTunes, where a colored bar shows you how much space is available and what types of file are currently using the capacity. This makes life a lot easier when you need to move or delete unnecessary files to make

room for your photographs. Just like on your computer, but at a more critical level due to the much smaller capacity, cleaning out unwanted files can save you valuable space, as can moving photos to Apple's iCloud.

Photographers get the most from the iPad when they combine the iPad's built-in storage space with a web-based facility, leaving you far more flexible when it comes to accessing and sharing your images. Many of the photographers we spoke to when putting together this book said they stored priority pictures on the iPad, and other shots on the web. Our favorite free web storing and sharing solution is DropBox, and is explained in detail at the end of this chapter.

SPACE AVAILABLE ON YOUR iPAD

Find out how much space is available on your iPad

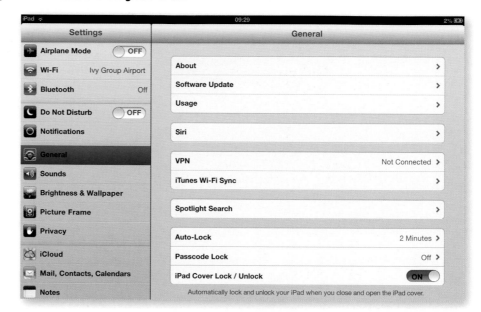

1 From the iPad's home screen, tap on the Settings app to launch it. Now tap on the General button.

2 From the list on the right of the General Settings screen, tap on About to find out more information regarding your iPad. The screen reveals how much of a type of media is on your iPad, the capacity of your device, and the available space. You're also shown how much space you have left in your iCloud backup space.

See what's taking up iPad space using iTunes

1 Start by connecting your iPad to your computer using the USB cable supplied with your device. If it hasn't launched automatically, load iTunes and select your iPad from the source panel on the left-hand side of the interface.

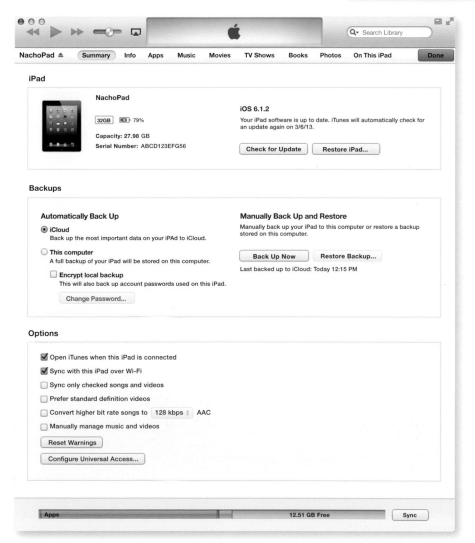

2 The screen that appears in the main iTunes window features a colored bar that shows the capacity being used by the different types of media on your device as well as the amount of free space.

TRANSFERRING FROM A CAMERA

Transferring photos from a camera

It's nothing new to be able to move pictures you've taken from a camera to a computer, and we're all used to this very simple process. The iPad is a different beast, however, and therefore does not offer the USB ports that allow for the direct transfer of photos from a camera to a hard drive. While most people would be content to transfer pictures from their camera to their computer and then sync them to their iPad, this doesn't necessarily work for the photographer, especially if they find themselves working in the field without a computer present. Luckily, Apple offers a way to skip the computer step with its Camera Connection Kit, which allows photos to be added to the iPad through a USB connection to the camera, or direct from an SD card. The iPad supports standard photo formats including JPEG and Raw files, so compatibility shouldn't be an issue, either.

Using the USB

The kit comes in two parts. One adapter connects to the dock connector port at the bottom of the iPad and then connects by way of a USB cable to a camera, while the second adapter allows for an SD card to be inserted and read through the connection kit. Once either of the two adapters are connected, the iPad's Photos app launches and shows all available images on the iPad's screen. You are then free to pick the images you want to import up to the size of your iPad's available space. When images are imported from a camera they are automatically organized into albums based on the metadata in each photograph. These images are then stored on the iPad, leaving you free to empty your camera's memory card and carry on shooting. This is an extremely handy feature if you're taking many shots or only have a small-capacity memory card to hand.

iPad as intermediary

While the transferred images remain on the iPad, they will be automatically transferred to your computer's photo library the next time you sync. Using the Camera Connection Kit, the iPad behaves as a useful intermediary between your camera and computer, offering more space for photos than a memory card, and a safe place to store images before they are transferred to your main library. It also gives you a way to show images to a client while on location or in the studio without having to hook up your camera or card to a computer. We'll cover sharing photos, along with tethered shooting, later on.

LEFT A USB-cable-to-iPad connector.

RIGHT An SD card reader.

Transfer photos from a camera to an iPad through USB

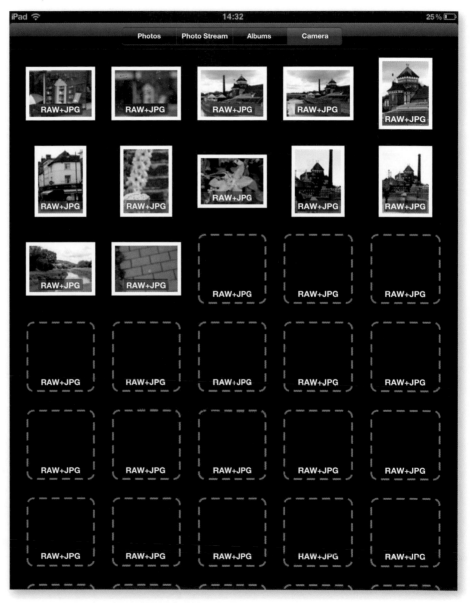

1 Connect Apple's Camera Connector part of the kit to your iPad using the Dock Connector on the bottom of the device. Now connect your camera to the USB cable and set your camera to transfer or hard-disk mode if it hasn't already done so automatically.

2 The Photos app will now quickly appear on your iPad as the device quickly downloads previews, from which you can select the photos you would like to import (or import all).

TRANSFERRING TO AN iPAD

Transfer photos to an iPad via SD card

1 Connect Apple's SD Card Reader to your iPad via the Dock Connector port.

2 Insert your SD Card into the Card Reader to launch the iPad's Photos app which will then read the SD Card.

3 Select the images you wish to transfer from the SD Card using the Photos app to save them to your iPad's photo library.

TRANSFERRING FROM A COMPUTER

Transferring photos from a computer

The quickest way to get your existing photographs onto your iPad is by syncing it with iTunes. You can sync photos in the same way you move applications, music, and movies to the device by simply connecting your iPad to your computer and letting iTunes do the work for you. Of course, you'll first need to tell it which photos you want to transfer and where they are stored. There are a number of different ways to perform photo syncing depending on the platform and software you are using, but once set up, your iPad will continue to be updated each time you plug it into your computer.

Syncing makes it easier to ensure you always have your latest and best photos with you, too. By selecting a specific folder on your hard drive, or in a desktop app like iPhoto or Aperture, you can add new images to it whenever you need to and they will be automatically transferred to your iPad the next time it's synced.

Another method, ideal for getting some pictures on your iPad quickly to show someone else, is to drag them into your PhotoStream, which is then shared to all your iCloud devices. You can do this in iPhoto, or on a Windows computer using the uploads folder you created when you set up iCloud (see page 12).

iTunes

RIGHT The iPad makes an ideal portable viewer for your images and offers slideshows to further enhance your shots.

IMPORTING FROM A MAC

Transferring photos to a MAC with iTunes

1 Connect your iPad to your computer using the provided USB cable. Connect one end to the iPad's dock connector socket and the other to an available USB slot on your computer. iTunes should now launch if it's not already open. If it doesn't launch automatically, do so manually. Now select your iPad from the source menu on the left of the iTunes interface.

2 Click on the Photos tab at the top of the screen and check the Sync Photos from box. Now just select the application in which you keep your photos from the pull-down menu. All of your albums and events should now be listed within iTunes for you to select. Choose to sync all photos, or a selection from your library, and click the Apply button to begin the transfer.

IMPORTING FROM A PC

Transferring photos to a PC with iTunes

1 Connect your iPad to your computer using the provided USB cable. Connect one end to the iPad's dock connector socket and the other to an available USB slot on your computer.

2 iTunes should now launch if it's not already open. If it isn't, launch it manually, then select your iPad from the source menu on the left of the iTunes interface.

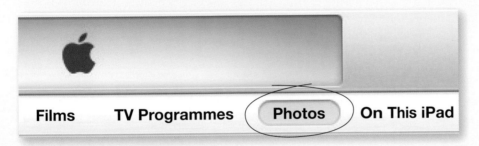

3 Click on the Photos tab at the top of the screen and check the Sync Photos from box. Now select Choose Folder from the pull-down menu.

4 Locate the directory in which your photos are stored and click on Select Folder to add it to the list. Now select individual folders of photos or select them all and click the Apply button to begin the transfer.

IMPORTING PHOTOS

Importing photos from email and the web

As well as a brilliant tool for viewing the web, the iPad also works as a great communication device, enabling you to connect to a range of email services. Attachments are also catered for with images appearing in-line in mail messages, or as a link, depending on how they were sent. You can, however, tell the iPad's Mail application not to download any images by turning the feature off through the iPad's Settings app. This is a useful technique if you're using a 3G/4G network, especially if you have a capped amount of usage every month. By preventing automatic downloads you can wait until you have a Wi-Fi connection to download, and you will also get faster downloads over a fixed broadband connection than you will over a mobile data network. Images that haven't been downloaded from the remote server will appear as a small icon, which, when tapped, will begin the download.

Zipped files and folders

Some mail clients may compress images sent to you through email, so remember that their quality may be reduced when viewing or displaying them to others. Mail clients may also archive large collections of images and send them as a compressed .ZIP-format file. The iPad does not offer native support for compressed formats like .ZIP so you will need a third-party application to access them from Mail on the iPad. The inexpensive app GoodReader adds support for archived files, as well as a number of popular formats that don't work natively on the iPad. However, Air Sharing HD also provides the facility and should be your preferred option given the additional features (see page 27).

Saving an image

The iPad has a built-in system for saving images. Simply hold a finger down on an image and select Save Image from the menu that appears. You can also choose Copy to save the image to the clipboard for pasting into an email or another document. Most images on the web can be stored this way, but you may find that some are embedded as part of the site or are built as a web link so you won't be able to store them. Don't panic. If you really need an image you find on the web, you can use the iPad's built-in screen-grabber. Zoom into the image on the web page using the pinch method, then press the iPad's Home button and the sleep/wake button at the same time. The screen will flash and you will hear the sound of a camera shutter. The image will then be stored in your photo library.

RIGHT Zipped files and folders.

BELOW importing photos from email.

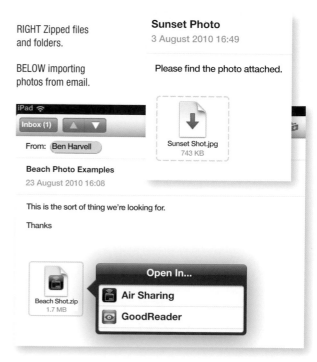

Save an image in an email to your iPad photo library

1 Start by opening the Mail app and selecting the message that contains the image you want to save.

2 If the image hasn't downloaded automatically, tap on the icon to begin downloading it. The progress of the download will be shown below the icon.

3 Once downloaded, the image will be displayed in the email message. Tap and hold your finger on the image until the menu shown appears. From the menu, tap on Save Image. The image will now be transferred to your photo library and can be accessed from the iPad's Photos app.

SHARING PHOTOS WIRELESSLY

One feature request common to many iPhone and iPad users is the ability to wirelessly sync and share files from their computer to their device. Apple hasn't provided such a feature yet, but a number of third-party app developers have stepped in to fill the gap. The benefit of wireless syncing over the traditional USB method is that updates can be made automatically without any action required on the user's part, just as emails are synced with a central server and sent to your iPad and your desktop computer. Wirelessly sharing photos makes the whole process that little bit easier than doing it manually.

Most applications that offer wireless sharing create a shared folder between the iPad and a computer, allowing images to be dragged from the desktop and automatically accessed on the iPad without the hassle of attaching the iPad to a computer and jumping into iTunes. To use these features, both the computer and the iPad will need to be connected to the Internet, and in some situations, connected to the same network. While there are many options available, the two options below offer the cleanest methods and use two different wireless sharing disciplines.

Avatron's Air Sharing HD creates a local folder on your computer to transfer images over a network, while Dropbox offers free online web

storage for your photos. You can access them on both your computer and the iPad and rely on the Dropbox software to keep both up-to-date. The method you choose depends on your circumstances and preferences when it comes to transferring files. If you're not happy to sync with iTunes every time you want to update the images on your iPad, then creating a wireless folder may not be for you. Remember though, that by using a web-based sharing option, you'll have access to these files wherever you have an Internet connection, not just at your desk. You'll hardly have to worry about syncing at all.

A final wireless sharing option is to make use of a special type of memory card called an Eye-Fi. Effectively a wireless SDHC card, the Eye-Fi and its corresponding software allows you to transfer images from a camera to a computer over the wireless network. For iPad users, the addition of a little piece of software called ShutterSnitch, easily found on the App Store, means you can apply the same technique with your iPad. With both your Eye-Fi card/Camera and iPad on the same wireless network, you simply tell ShutterSnitch your Eye-Fi username and password and it will grab images from the card and add them to your iPad.

RIGHT The Eye-Fi card offers a clever way to send photos directly from a camera to a connected device.

Shuttersnitch

AIR SHARING HD

Air Sharing HD is a powerful app that enables you to take your photos and documents with you on your iPad with a minimum of fuss. Any Mac, Windows, or Linux computer can mount an Air Sharing HD as a wireless hard disk, making it easy to drag files between your computer desktop and the Air Sharing HD volume. Then you can view documents, transfer files between file servers, print documents wirelessly, and manage your files. The app can connect to a wide variety of file servers, including Dropbox, FTP or FTPS, SFTP (SSH File Transfer Protocol), and WebDAV. If you are familiar with Apple's Finder or Windows Explorer, Air Sharing HD's interface will feel very familiar. File and folder icons are presented on a desktop-style interface with folders for categorizing your documents. You can even browse into ZIP archives without uncompressing—a major bonus given that the iPad doesn't offer support for the ZIP format.

For photographers, Air Sharing HD's support for very high-resolution photos is a welcome feature. The iPad's built-in Photos app is a great image viewer, but it has been known to have issues when it comes across high-res images. Unlike Photos, you can also drag files easily and wirelessly into Air Sharing HD's folder hierarchy without having to sync your iPad to commit each transfer. Keeping your iPad mounted on your desktop with Air Sharing HD means that, even if you have to rush out, you can quickly drag your images to your iPad without having to sync all the other media stored on it, such as music, movies, and podcasts.

Air Sharing HD

RIGHT Sharing files wirelessly to your iPad isn't as tricky as it might sound, especially with apps like Air Sharing HD.

Drop Box

AIR SHARING HD ON A MAC

Connect and share photos with Air Sharing HD on a Mac

1 Open your iPad's Settings app and then Select Wi-Fi. Now pick the wireless network used by your computer from the list.

2 Now launch Air Sharing HD and tap on the wrench at the bottom right of the interface to bring up the settings menu. Tap on Sharing Security.

3 Add a name and password for your iPad to make sure it's secure when sharing wirelessly. You can also add a passcode to lock the application for additional security.

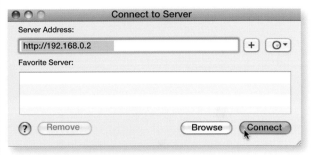

4 Turn on the Allow Sleep option to avoid communication problems if your device goes to sleep while mounted.

5 On your Mac, click on the desktop to make sure you are in the Finder and hit Apple+K to pick a server to connect to. The address you need for your iPad can be found in the Help section of the Air Sharing HD app under Mac OS X. Type in the IP address given and enter a password if required. Your iPad should now mount as a drive on your desktop.

Name	Date Modified	Size	Kind
IMG_0315.JPG	20 August 2010 10:03	90 KB	JPEG image
Inbox	3 August 2010 16:37	--	Folger
photo.JPG	20 August 2010 10:03	118 KB	JPEG image
Public	14 May 2010 15:46	--	Folder
Samples	9 April 2010 13:17	--	Folder
Snaps	20August 2010 10:03	--	Folder
Snaps.zip	1 January 1970 01:30	311 KB	Zip archive

6 Files can now be transferred to and from your iPad by way of your desktop by adding images to the mounted folder. Try dragging the folder to your Dock to access quickly in future.

AIR SHARING HD USING WINDOWS

Connect and share photos with Air Sharing HD using Windows Vista/Windows 7

1 Follow steps 1 to 4 above, then open Windows Explorer and select Map Network Drive from the top of the window. Click on the Folder field of the My Network Drive window and enter the IP address or Bonjour name of your iPad. Click Finish and you should be connected.

2 If you don't know the IP address or Bonjour name of your iPad, you can find this info in Air Sharing HD by tapping the Wi-Fi symbol in the menu bar at the bottom.

Connect and share photos with Air Sharing HD using Windows XP

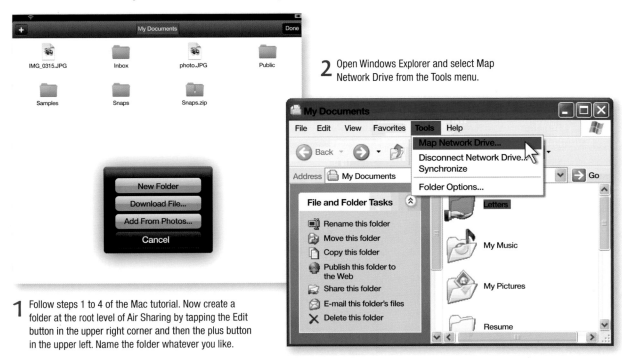

2 Open Windows Explorer and select Map Network Drive from the Tools menu.

1 Follow steps 1 to 4 of the Mac tutorial. Now create a folder at the root level of Air Sharing by tapping the Edit button in the upper right corner and then the plus button in the upper left. Name the folder whatever you like.

3 In the Folder field of the window that comes up, enter the IP address or Bonjour name of your iPad as listed in Air Sharing HD followed by the name of the folder you just created. For example, http://10.0.1.1/Documents. Click Finish and you should be connected.

USING DROPBOX

Using Dropbox

Dropbox is a free service designed to allow users to share files and folders across multiple computers and mobile devices, including the iPad. Dropbox effectively provides a single shared folder online, and all connected devices can access and edit this folder's contents, making it an ideal place to store your photos. The software constantly monitors your Dropbox folder and updates all devices connected to it accordingly. Edit a photo that is stored in your Dropbox folder using your computer, and the next time you access the same image on your iPad by way of Dropbox, it will show all the edits you made at your last visit. Similarly, if you're heading out to visit a client and you're taking your iPad, you can quickly drop relevant images into your Dropbox folder and they will be accessible as and when you need them. After signing up for an account at www.dropbox.com, you will have access to 2GB of storage, which should be more than enough for a few albums worth. If you need more, you just have to pay a monthly or annual fee.

Dropbox can be installed on as many computers as you desire, and all you need for your iPad is the free Dropbox app from the iTunes Store. Images opened from within the Dropbox iPad app can be transferred to the iPad's photo library or opened in another iPad application if required. The bonus here is that, whether you're using your desktop computer, a laptop, or your iPad, you can access the same library of images and make changes that will be reflected on each device you use.

The Dropbox app is universal too, so it can be used on an iPhone as well as your iPad. In addition to providing a unique way to access images on the iPad, Dropbox offers a number of additional benefits. Everything within your Dropbox folder is automatically backed up online, for example, offering you extra peace of mind, and you can also provide a link to your Dropbox to other users so that they can look at your images and be notified when you make changes. These collaboration options make it an ideal tool for photographers working in groups or for receiving feedback from clients with changes and updates to files in your Dropbox made almost instantly. When using Dropbox on the iPad, you do need to have an Internet connection to access your files but, if you think you might be caught short, Dropbox offers a Favorites feature that stores Dropbox files on your iPad for offline use.

Dropbox

Share photos with Dropbox

2 Follow the instructions to set up your account and access your Dropbox folder on your computer. Locate the Dropbox folder on your computer. This can be found in the User folder or via the menu bar on a Mac, and on a Windows system in the system tray or via the Start menu.

1 Download and install Dropbox for your computer from www.dropbox.com, then visit the App Store and download the App for your iPad.

3 Select the images or folders you wish to add to your Dropbox folder and drag them into it. These images will now be available on all of your devices that have Dropbox running.

4 Launch the Dropbox iPad app and enter your Dropbox login details. Now press the button at the top left of the interface to access your Dropbox. Select the images you wish to view or the folder containing them. From this view you can flick through your images or save them to your iPad's Photos app. You can even email a link to your Dropbox images if you wish.

EDITING PHOTOS

Out of the box, the iPad doesn't have any image-editing tools available when accessing images from its photo library. While images can be viewed and shared, even the most basic of adjustments must be performed using a computer. There are, however, a great number of third-party applications that, for a minimal cost, will provide at least some of the editing options provided by desktop applications like Adobe Photoshop and Apple's Aperture. While no sensible photographer should give up their desktop-based editing suite for an iPad, the option to edit images in the field and quickly fire them out to clients and colleagues by way of email is of serious benefit. The iPad's display is also ideal for the task and, in many respects, better than a laptop screen or the LCD display found on a camera or preview device. Editing on the iPad can also boost your workflow, providing a chance to make adjustments while traveling between a location and the studio, or during any downtime.

"better than a laptop display or LCD display found on a camera"

In this chapter the focus is on two iPad photo-editing apps—one you'll have heard of and the other a relative unknown. Photoshop Express is Adobe's free photo-editing tool for iPad and offers some fairly basic features, but balances these limitations with its web-based capabilities that allow for sharing photos and online storage through a photoshop.com account, which you may already have set up. Photogene is an independent iPad image editor that offers a great range of features for a minimal fee. The two apps have their own merits and you'll have to sample both to find the one that's right for you, though the Photoshop Express's zero cost is a major selling point. Over the next few pages you will learn how to perform basic image edits with Photogene for iPad and how to access and adjust your photoshop.com images with Photoshop Express.

Photoshop Express

Photogene

RIGHT Inexpensive yet powerful, Photogene is a useful addition to your iPad's image-editing arsenal.

PHOTOSHOP EXPRESS

If you already use Adobe's photoshop.com, then Photoshop for the iPad is the ideal partner. If you're not using photoshop.com, why not? The popular online service allows you to share, edit, and host images, with 2GB of space for your photos and videos with a free account (and expandable for a price—it's worth checking out Adobe's subscription policies as there are some good deals, particularly if you're updating. Photoshop Express is the natural extension of this service on the iPad, allowing you to make use of the plethora of features on the site using your iPad and it also ties in with the Adobe Apps on your desktop, providing another way to transfer and access your photos on the move.

The photoshop.com upload makes adding photos and video to your account a cinch, thanks to simply drag and drop functionality. Set your albums to sync to your photoshop.com and you'll always be up to date. When you've stored photos on photoshop.com, simply log-in to the Photoshop Express app to view, edit and share your images, straight from your iPad. You can even upload shots from your iPad to photoshop.com, so edits you do in the field can you live on the service within minutes. Photoshop Express on the iPad creates a unique workflow for your images and allows you to edit wherever you are, safe in the knowledge that any file you edit on the move will be updated and ready for review when you return to your desk. Photoshop Express is free from the iTunes App Store.

Accessing photos from www.photoshop.com

1 Assuming you haven't already, visit www.photoshop.com and register for a free account. Use the web interface to upload any images you want to make available for editing.

2 Launch Photoshop Express on your iPad and tap the Online button at the bottom of the interface and enter your photoshop.com username and password to log in to your account.

3 As your photoshop.com account is synced with Photoshop Express on your iPad you'll now be able to see the photographs you uploaded to the website in your library.

4 Tap on an image thumbnail to load it and swipe left and right to see more of the image in you library.

Edit and share your photographs

1 Launch the Photoshop Express app and tap the Edit button at the bottom of the interface. Tap the Select Photo button and pick an image from your library or any imported albums on your iPad.

2 Your image will now open in within the editing interface. Use the second tool from the bar across the bottom for basic edits as needed: Crop, Straighten, Rotate and Flip.

3 Next, explore the last three tools, to alter exposure, color and add effects and boarders. If you try something you don't like, simply click Undo. When you make an adjustment you're happy with tap the tick button that appears in the bottom right.

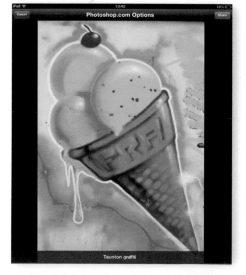

4 When you're done editing your image, you can send it straight to your photoshop.com account by tapping the Share button in the top left, then picking the Photoshop logo from the bar along the button. Add a caption and choose an album, if you like, then click share in the top right. Share by email, Facebook, twitter or tumbler using the corresponding buttons.

PHOTOSHOP EXPRESS

Adding effects to your photographs with Photoshop Express

1 Open the Photoshop Express app and tap the Edit button at the bottom of the interface. Tap the Select Photo button and pick an image from your library or any imported albums on your iPad.

2 Before you get started with effects do any basic edits, like cropping and altering exposure, using the first three controls along the tool bar at the bottom of the interface.

3 From the tool bar, select the forth tool along and try out the Colorize control. Get duo tone effects by simply sliding your finger up and down, through the different colors. Tap the tick in the bottom right when happy.

4 Tap the fifth tool along with stars. Tap the first effect then use your finger to slide through all the free effects available to you. If you find one you like, tap the tick in the bottom right.

Lens Zoom Blur

5 Try the plethora of other effects you'll see with a dollar sign in the top right-hand corner. These 45 effects make up the Adobe Effects Pack, which costs £1.99. Try before you decide if you want to buy.

PURCHASE ADOBE EFFECT PACK

• Give your photos fun, fresh looks using more than 45 eye-catching effects.
• Adjust effects with simple dragging motions.
• Preview effects on your photos before you apply them.

Learn more online

Close   Buy

6 We're pretty sure you'll see several effects you love—which would take hours to create from scratch in Photoshop. Assuming you want to purchase the Adobe Effects Pack, click the shopping cart in the bottom right, tap buy and confirm your purchase through the iTunes Store.

7 All the dollar signs will now disappear from the effects and you're free to use them as much as you like. To share the images you've created, tap the Share button, then choose email, Photoshop.com, Facebook, twitter or tumbler, using the corresponding buttons.

Created with the Lens Zoom effect

Created with the Colorize palette

Created with the Vintage II effect

Created with the free Vignette Blur filter

PHOTOGENE FOR iPAD

Photogene for iPad, developed by Omer Shoor, is in our opinion, presently the best all-round editing solution for the iPad. If you like to have one suite, which does everything and with ease, Photogene is for you. This app deals with all the important editing tasks and handles them with ease—whether it's simple red eye removal or putting together large collages. The array of tools it offers are impressive and it can open up for editing very large files and supports an export resolution of up to 21 MP. The pictures you edit using Photogene can be synced back to your computer from the iPad for further editing, printing or publishing.

Photogene's Metadata Viewer provides a detailed visual display of all the information stored in your photos. As well as viewing complete EXIF metadata and where the photo was taken on a map, you can also view and edit IPTC metadata, which allows you to input your details as the photographer, copyright information and a caption. Access is gained via the Metadata in the top right-hand corner of the Photogene editing screen.

1 Open an image you want to adjust exposure and color on, buy clicking the Photogene icon in the top left and viewing the images you've imported onto, or taken with, your iPad.

2 Select adjustments from the tool bar on the bottom of the screen—a menu with several tools will now appear on the right-hand side. You'll see there are slider controls covering color, exposure and contrast.

3 In the Adjustments menu, scroll down to the bottom and open the Curves menu. Pull the curve line around the picture until you have the exposure you want.

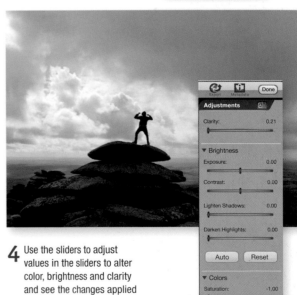

4 Use the sliders to adjust values in the sliders to alter color, brightness and clarity and see the changes applied in real time to the image in the main window.

PHOTOGENE FOR iPAD

Retouch your portraits

1 Open the image you want to work on, by clicking the Photogene icon in the top left and viewing the images you've imported onto, or taken with, your iPad.

2 Using your fingers, zoom into the picture, so you have a detailed look at the area(s) you want to retouch.

3 Select the Retouches option from the bottom of the screen. A menu with all the different tools and masks will now appear on the right-hand side. To rid your photograph of any blemishes or restore damaged areas, select the Heal tool.

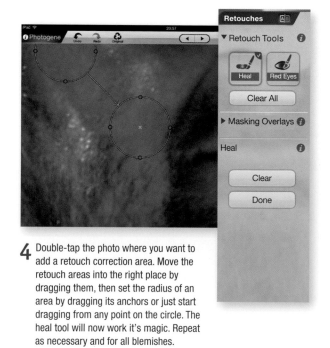

4 Double-tap the photo where you want to add a retouch correction area. Move the retouch areas into the right place by dragging them, then set the radius of an area by dragging its anchors or just start dragging from any point on the circle. The heal tool will now work it's magic. Repeat as necessary and for all blemishes.

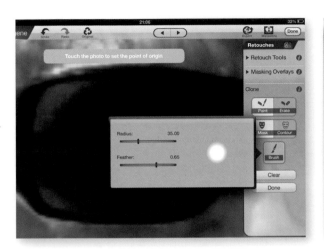

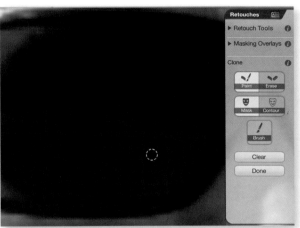

5 Select the Clone tool from the menu on the right, then select Paint and Mask from the options. Press the brush button and then choose a radius and feather value that suits the area you're getting rid of.

6 Double tap on the area you'd like the clone tool to sample from, then use your finger as a brush the paint away your unwanted object.

Before

7 When you're finished perfecting your portrait—you might want to use other tools such as read eye correction—simply press Done in the top right and your image will be saved in your Photo Stream.

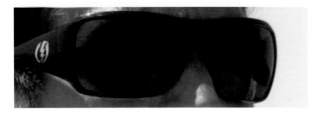

After

Together, Photogene's Adjustments mode and Retouches mode give you everything you need to make sophisticated portrait edits straight from your iPad.

FILTERSTORM

Filterstorm has been designed from the ground up to meet your iPad (and iPhone) photo editing needs and that shows when you use it. The interface allows for intuitive editing and it boast a toolset suited to serious photographers, rather than gimmicky effects. For editing on the go, you'll find Filterstorm has everything you could need in an editing suite including layers, curves manipulation, color correction abilities, noise reduction, sharpening, vignetting, and black and white conversion fine-tuning. Impressively the app also allows you to adjust masks by brush, color range, gradient, and vignettes.

See Filterstorm's website at www.filterstorm.com for support, videos and tutorials.

Filterstorm 4
Retouching Images With Your Touch.

Small Device, Big Power

Filterstorm was designed from the ground up to meet your mobile photo editing needs. Using a uniquely crafted touch interface, Filterstorm allows for more intuitive editing than its desktop counterparts with a toolset designed for serious photorgaphy.

Main

Features

Videos

Automations

IPTC Support

FSPro2 vs. FS4

Support

Tutorials

Purchase

FS Pro

Blog

Twitter

Filterstorm contains a suite of pwerful tools including curves manipulation, color correction abilities, noise reduction, unsharp masking, and black and white conversion fine-tuning. Its powerful

1 Import the photo you'd like to tone map into Filterstorm using the Load Photo button—you can select from anywhere on your iPad.

2 Do any preliminary basic edits like straightening and cropping in the Canvas menu, then select the Filters and choose Tone Mapping.

3 Using the Radius and Strength sliders on the left-hand side add the effect, being careful not to overcook your image.

4 You may want to add a border to your tone mapped image as we've done here— simply select the Canvas menu again, select Borders, then input your preferences.

5 When you're finished editing you'll no doubt want to share your image. To export, click on the icon of an arrow within a box, in the top right, select your preferences, and then click Export.

iPHOTO

If you're looking for an image-editing suite for your iPad that combines power with ease of use, you'll love iPhoto. Intuitive and fun to use, you can get professional looking edits in minutes. Imagine making your sky bluer using just your fingers, in a few seconds! iPhoto will certainly change the way you edit your images in your iPad and undoubtedly make your workflow quicker. You're bound to love the app's swatch book—dozens of beautifully designed photo effects ranging from dramatic to dreamy, applied within a blink of an eye.

iPhoto gives you a great view of your images. The scrollable thumbnail grid lets you glide through your pictures in either portrait or landscape. You can also compare pictures side by side, mark your favorites and hide those you're not so keen on.

MULTI-TOUCH EDITING As soon as you're selected an image, you can immediately start making the best of it by adjusting exposure, contrast, saturation and color channels—simply touch the paint palette icon in the bottom left hand corner and then click on the area of your image you'd like to adjust and an icon with four arrows will appear. Simply slide your finger in the direction of the effect you want to add, sliding further for more intensity. Voilà!

ADDING EFFECTS If you've always fancied duotone images or want to add a black-and-white filter, you'll love the professional edit effects iPhoto provides you with—there are dozens to choose from. To access the swatch book, touch the stars icon in the bottom left hand corner, and then use the swatches to change the look and feel of your photo. Then pinch, zoom or slide to adjust an effect, so it's perfect. "It took me hours, honest."

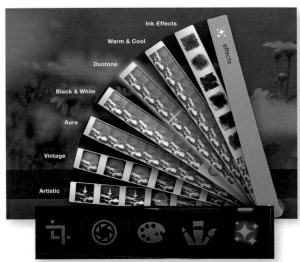

MULTI-TOUCH EDITING With iPhoto's brushes, touch-ups are literally that—selecting a brush and then using your finger to paint the effect on. Available brushes are Repair (great for getting rid of blemishes), Red Eye, Saturate, Desaturate, Lighten, Darken, Sharpen (bring out fine details) and Soften (smooth any hard lines and edges that offend you). Zoom in, using your fingers, so you can see the area you're working on up close. Magic.

SNAPSEED

The developers at Nik software have given us a real treat with Snapseed; developed from the ground up as a touch app, it boasts a unique and extremely intuitive interface. You have to be willing to invest a little of your time learning how it works, but as soon as you do you'll be able to give your images creative new looks, that look like you've spent an age editing them on your PC, not within a few minutes on your iPad! It's important to recognize that Snapseed isn't just a toy to use with the iPad's built-in camera—it's a powerful piece of software, that allows you to the exploit the extra bit depth from your DSLR's RAW files to create truly inspirational and creative edits, without the need for a computer, ready to go in your portfolio or shared with friends and clients. Amazingly, Snapseed is free.

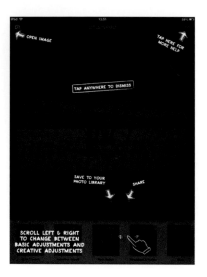

ABOVE Although using Snapseed is intuitive, it does work differently from the bars and sliders of Photoshop et al, so you'll need to be prepared to learn a new way of working. Luckily, the welcome screen helps you out with these handy pointers.

Applying a Grunge Look

2 Slide the adjustments pane on the right-hand side and choose Grunge from the options. As you do, you're image will go full screen, so you can get to work.

1 Choose Open Image in the top left and select an image from those you've copied across from you camera, which you would like to work with.

3 With one finger, tap and drag up or down on the screen. A menu will appear, and the menu highlighted when you let go (which can be seen in the gauge at the bottom of the screen also) is the one you can then edit. Select Style then simply stroke your finger to the right to increase the strength of the effect.

4 When you're happy and want to accept the change, click on the Apply button in the lower right.

5 Now repeat steps 3 and 4, but selecting Brightness, Contrast, Texture Strength and finally Saturation, making your adjustments for each by sliding to the right and pressing the Apply button as before.

6 The center-point of your focus effect is indicated by a blue dot. With your finger, simply drag it to where you want your picture's new focal point. Press Apply for a final time and then use the Share button to show others.

Final image

DESKTOP EDITING SOFTWARE

Working with desktop editing software and the iPad

The iPad works nicely with most of the major photo-editing and organization tools on both Mac and PC. Adobe's Lightroom and Apple's Aperture provide the cleanest ways to work between iPad and desktop when it comes to import and export, with both able to "see" the iPad and the photos it contains. As discussed in the chapter on importing photos, images from applications that do not automatically link to the iPad when it is connected to a computer can still be transferred back and forth using iTunes. If you are using Adobe's Creative Suite you can also import iPad images to Adobe Bridge through the Adobe Photo Downloader. This will make them available for use in any of the Creative Suite applications.

If you intend to edit the images you import from your iPad, it's best to remove them from the iPad after you've moved them to your computer, as otherwise you may get duplicates. Most applications that can import images from your iPad will also offer the option to delete the imported images after transfer. Once edited, these images can be transferred back to your iPad using iTunes in the normal way.

Extending your screen with Air Display

When you are working with photos on your desktop in applications like Photoshop, Light Room, or Aperture, your iPad can still be involved in the process. Using a number of third-party applications, you can add some real estate to your computer screen with your iPad by using it as an additional monitor. With the iPad docked next to your computer and an app like Air Display running, the screen of your iPad continues your desktop space and can be configured to appear on the left or right of the screen in landscape or portrait orientation. The connection between your iPad and computer is made through Wi-Fi, so you don't have to worry about additional cables. While the quality of display on your iPad when sharing screens isn't quite as good as the real thing, it still adds a handy bit of room for applications or folders that would otherwise clutter up your screen.

Even better, Air Display allows you to interact with items on the iPad screen using the touch interface, enabling you to move windows and control apps without having to move your cursor to the second screen. For photographers, this method offers some serious benefit, especially when using applications with tool palettes like Photoshop. By grouping all of your palettes onto the iPad screen you can use all of your desktop space to work on an image, tapping the required tools as you need them. Air Display will also dramatically improve the screen area of a laptop, in some cases doubling it, when the iPad is used as a second display.

Extend your computer's screen with Air Display and an iPad

1 Make sure your iPad and computer both have Wi-Fi turned on and are connected to the same wireless network.

2 Download and install the Air Display support software from www.Avatron.com/ad, then launch it to configure your system.

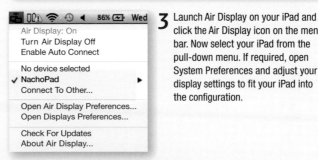

3 Launch Air Display on your iPad and click the Air Display icon on the menu bar. Now select your iPad from the pull-down menu. If required, open System Preferences and adjust your display settings to fit your iPad into the configuration.

4 SHOOTING AIDS

As well as the obvious benefits the iPad provides when it comes to viewing, sharing, and editing images, it also offers a wealth of useful features when shooting. For a start, the iPad is a very portable device that can easily be slung into a camera bag without adding as much weight as a laptop to your already heavy selection of kit. Second, as it's pretty much all screen, the iPad makes an ideal preview tool when using it tethered to your camera. In fact, with a 2048 x 1536 retina display and 4:3 aspect ratio, images will be displayed more accurately than on some laptop screens. Then there's the rest of the iPad's built-in features to consider, the organizational powers of the Calendar app, plus email access and Maps.

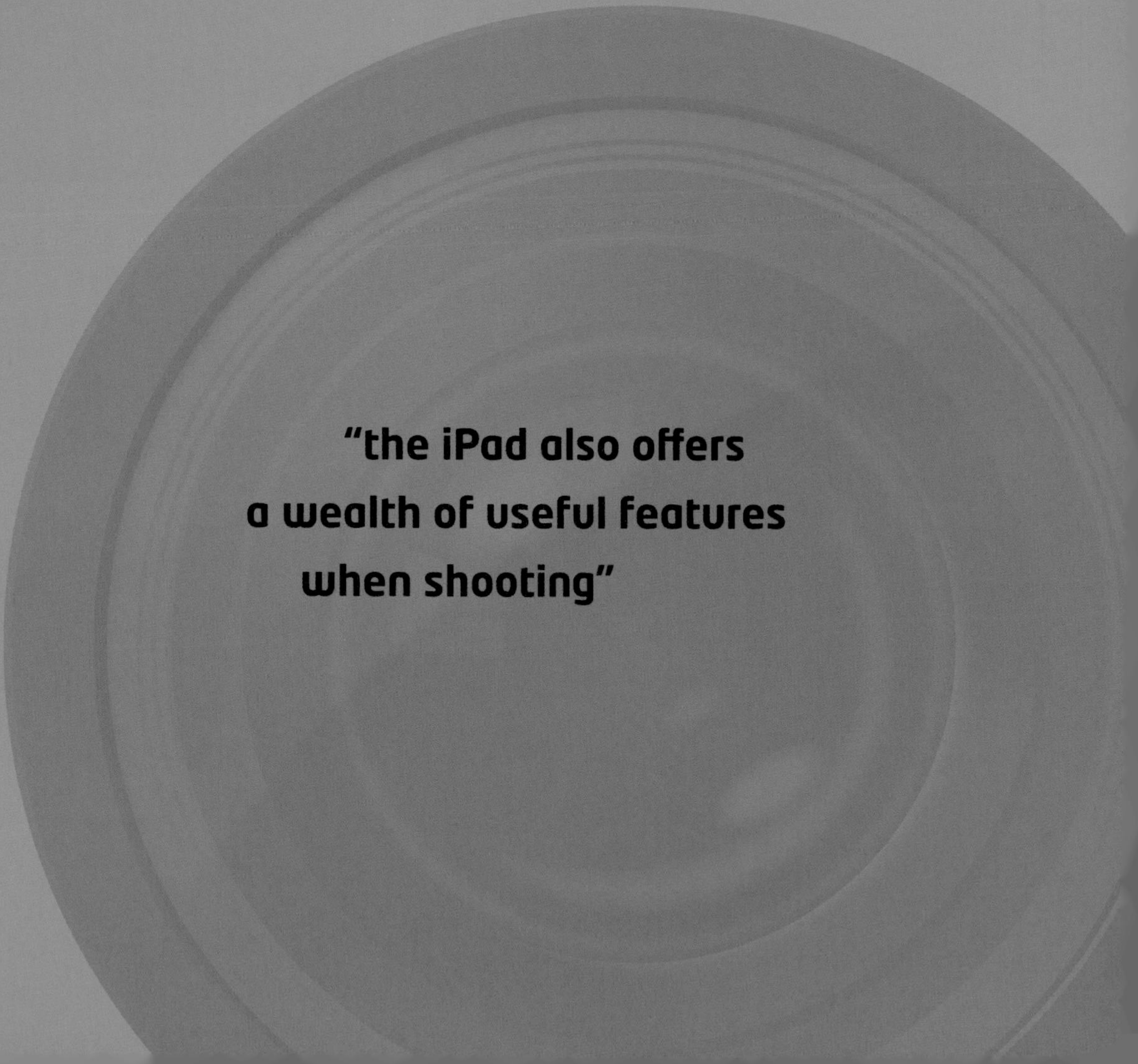

"the iPad also offers
a wealth of useful features
when shooting"

With a web connection, not only does the iPad provide a unique way to get instant feedback on the images you take, it also enables you to share them and stay on top of the admin at the same time. There are many great applications available on the App Store that will be perfect for your organizational requirements, but for the duration of this chapter, the focus is mainly on the apps you already have. Some features do require a web connection, so if you're not using a 3G iPad or a mobile hotspot, you may not be able to make use of all of them. However, if you also have an iPhone, it can fill in for your iPad when you're away from a Wi-Fi connection. Later in the book, we'll look at some examples of ideal applications that will add even more features to your iPad, but for now let's take a look at the ways in which you can organize, plan, and even geotag your photos.

Mail

1. Charge batteries
2. Plan route to shoot
3. Send location to attendees
4. Update budget
5. Book studio

Calendar

Google Maps

RIGHT As well as performing as a photography tool, the iPad can also serve as a perfect digital organizer. This is ideal for photographers looking to keep track of shoots, deadlines, and other events.

:SHOOTING AIDS

Planning and workflow

With a suite of organizational tools coming as standard with the iPad, you won't be short of ways to stay on top of your day-to-day tasks. The main contenders here are the email, calendar, and map tools, which all work beautifully together to help your workflow run smoothly. For an inexpensive and effective way to keep all of your information in sync, try using Google's family of tools, which includes a calendar and email, plus online office applications. These apps and services are available for free, and you can sign up for them via www.google.com. What's more, Google's services are compatible with all the iPad's corresponding apps; a Google Mail™ account can be synced with the Mail app, while contacts from your Google account can be synced with the Contacts app. Google's online Calendar can be synced with the Calendar app and the iPad's Maps app is actually powered by the Google Maps™ service. Even Notes can be synced to multiple accounts if you wish.

You can access all of these services directly from the Google website, but by adding the accounts to your iPad you can keep all your vital information in sync from wherever you are. The same services work with apps on your computer, further extending their usefulness.

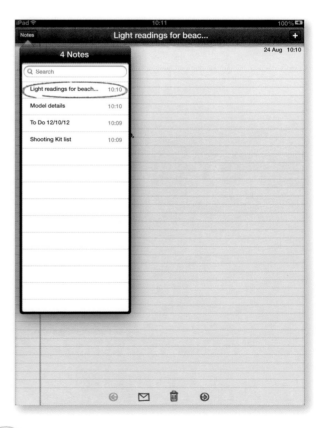

ABOVE The iPad's built-in Notes application is perfect for jotting down information when you're shooting in the field.

Working with email, your calendar, and the Maps app

Let's say a client has commissioned you to perform a shoot at a location you've never visited before. You need to find where you're supposed to be going, keep in touch with the team you're working with, and cost the shoot as you go. The date is in your iPad's calendar, be it Google or Yahoo!, and the appointment can be shared with all of those involved. You take your iPad with you so you can use the Maps application to quickly locate where you're headed and even get directions. If you're meeting others at the shoot, perhaps models or assistants, you can then email the exact location to them from the Maps application, and they will then be able to view this through Google Maps on any web-connected device they use. With the Notes app you can quickly check off a list of "to do" items both before and during the shoot, and share this list by way of email.

There are also a number of third-party "to do" list apps on the App Store that offer a more detailed set of features for organizing just such an event. During the shoot you can keep others informed of your progress, track new locations,

store the coordinates by way of the Maps app, record light readings and timing information, and even use Apple's Numbers or a Google Documents™ spreadsheet to add last-minute expenses to your budget. Whether you use the iPad's default tools or buy others from the App Store (find out which are essential in the chapter on must-have apps), the iPad offers all the flexibility of a laptop, and more, without the additional bulk. Even without a web connection, the iPad is perfectly capable of storing the information you enter into it offline, ready to be shared when you next have Internet access.

ABOVE The Maps application offers a handy way to plan your route and allows you to use GPS coordinates.

©2010 Google—Map data ©2011 Maplink, Tele Atlas, Imagery ©2011 NASA, Terrametrics

TETHERED SHOOTING

It's not a well-known fact, but the iPad can also be used as a display for tethered shooting. It's a little more fiddly than the traditional method of connecting a camera to a laptop or desktop computer but, once you have it configured, it's a great way to show pictures to others as they are being taken. In fact, you can even use the iPad to trigger the shot if you want. Both of the methods described below require additional software and will also need a laptop or desktop computer to work, so it's not true iPad tethering, but it's still a neat trick nonetheless. Hopefully, an app will provide support for true tethering in the near future, but for now the best options are to use Air Display HD as an external monitor and control, or use an Eye-Fi card and Apple's Camera Connection Kit with the ShutterSnitch App.

Tethered shooting using Air Display

This method is probably the simplest of the two to set up, but will require you to already be using tethering software on your computer or laptop. When testing this setup, I found Adobe's Lightroom to be the best tool for the tethering job, but feel free to experiment with your preferred software. First up, you'll need a copy of Air Display from Avatron Software, the same app mentioned in the section on desktop editing earlier in the book. You will also need compatible tethering software such as Adobe's Light Room (or any tethering app that came with your camera) running while you take your shots, as well as the free desktop components for the Air Display software.

Effectively what is happening using this technique is that the tethering application on your computer is displayed on the iPad's screen wirelessly. The image quality isn't incredible, but it does allow you to view the shot you've just taken and even trigger the camera using the iPad's interface. The technique still requires a computer or laptop, but it does add an additional screen into the mix, meaning you can have your laptop or desktop computer working as your preview and give the iPad to someone else to monitor shots wirelessly from anywhere within range of your Wi-Fi network.

1 Launch Air Display on your iPad and your computer.

2 Set the desktop application to Mirror Displays so you see the same on your computer screen as you do on your iPad.

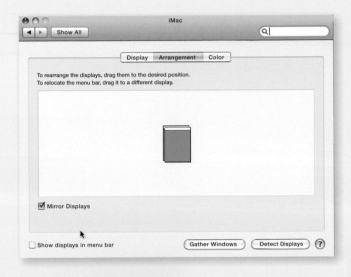

3 Launch your chosen tethering application and bring it up to full screen. Configure the application so that it's ready to be tethered to your camera.

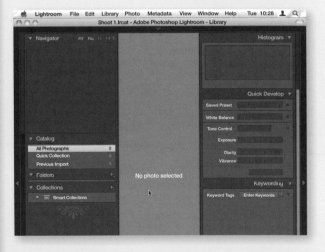

4 Connect your camera to your computer as usual and position it ready for shooting with a tripod. Shoot your images manually or using on-screen tools using the iPad or your laptop. While you are shooting you can mount your iPad or give it to others to view the shots as they are taken.

:TETHERED SHOOTING

Tethered shooting using an Eye-Fi card

Another way to capture images from a camera using your iPad is by using a wireless memory card called an Eye-Fi. This card can connect by way of Wi-Fi to a computer or, in this case, an iPad, and transfer the images stored on it. By using an application called ShutterSnitch, the iPad can show the images stored to the card on its screen each time a picture is taken, making it ideal for setting up shots or for showing work in progress to models and clients while you shoot. In order to make this technique work you will need a camera that is compatible with the Eye-Fi card, a copy of the ShutterSnitch app, and a wireless network to connect to. You could create an *ad hoc* wireless network using a mobile Wi-Fi router, but this is ideally a technique for a studio where an existing wireless network is in place.

Geotagging

Geotagging, or the process of adding GPS coordinates to the metadata of an image, is becoming increasingly popular. It makes sense for photographers to make use of the technology to organize galleries and record favorite shooting locations. A number of popular cameras from major manufacturers come with a built-in GPS chip that records location data for each photo, and there are also a number of devices that can be carried on the photographer's person, or attached to a DSLR, that perform the same task. If you have an iPhone 3G or above, you can even download an application to record GPS locations while you shoot. Most non-built-in options require additional software to match coordinates to photos after shooting and this normally comes bundled with the devices themselves.

Geotagging is especially important to iPad users as it means that they can make use of the Places feature found in the Photos app to sort their images by location. Within the Photos app, tapping on the Places button at the top of the display shows a world map with thumbtacks placed at locations where photos have been taken. The app uses the metadata included in geotagged photos to position them on the map, and this provides a handy way to sort your images by country or place. The iPhone and iPad camera records GPS data with each image taken, which can come in handy on shoots or location scouting. Simply snap a quick reference shot and your location will be logged. As an alternative to the above methods, if you don't have an iPad or an iPhone, you can also use your iPad to record basic GPS information while you're shooting by using the Maps application to find your current location. You can then send the information in an email to yourself or your colleagues so that you can add it to the metadata of photos for organizing later.

Geotag

LEFT An Eye-Fi card can connect via Wi-Fi to your iPad.

Store your GPS location using an iPad

1 Start by launching the Maps application from your iPad's home screen. Now tap on the arrow button at the top of the interface to pinpoint your current location.

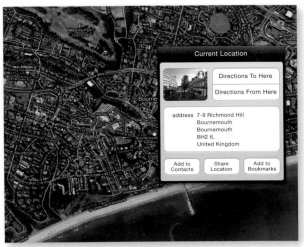

2 A small blue dot will appear on the map with a red thumbtack. Tap on the dot and then tap on the blue "I" button that appears next to it.

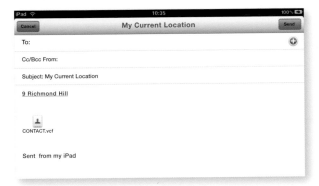

3 Now tap on Share Location in the box that appears to send the location in an email. Add your own address in the To: field and tap on send.

4 When your email arrives, the first line will include a link that, when clicked, will open in Google Maps on a computer and in the Maps application on the iPad. The GPS location will be included in the search field.

BENEFITS OF IPAD CAMERAS

Your iPad's camera is never going to be a threat to your DSLR, or even your top packet camera, but it's still a good tool and adds to the tablet's functionality. The camera was a very welcome addition when introduced with the iPad 2, even though it was just 0.7 MP. Luckily, Apple's iPad camera offering has come a long way since then, with the third and forth generation models and the iPad mini all equipped a 5MP camera, complete with 5x digital zoom and 30fps shooting speed—nothing compared to your DSLR and probably more compatible to your phone's camera. However, it is incredibly useful having a camera built into your iPad—they're great for grabbing reference shots and capturing behind the scenes photos to share on social media or via email.

The option to record video is incredibly useful too, for instance, when you're scouting for locations, it's sometimes easier to shoot a video to use as reference, rather than a series of pictures. Or, a behind the scenes video of a fashion shoot would probably go down a treat on Facebook.

Shooting with the iPad is as simple as just tapping the Camera icon on your iPad's home screen and pointing your devise, in the same way you would with a point-and-shoot camera. Switching between photo and video is done simply by sliding between the still and video mode icons at the bottom of the screen.

A great benefit of your iPad's camera is the FaceTime feature, which enables you to make video calls between compatible Apple devises—other iPads, iPhones, iPod touches and Macs. You will need Wi Fi to use FaceTime, but a Mi Fi device will work when you're on location or away from your home or office connection. Video calling can add a greater level of communication to your work, allowing you to show off locations, set-ups and styling to clients and directors, almost as if they were there with you—great for feedback.

Lastly, on the front of your iPad you'll find a Photo Booth app, which more than anything is a great bit of fun. Unless you're in the market for novelty images, we doubt you'll use it for any serious work—but it may well provide you will a valuable tool for entertaining bored children on shoots, or making them crack a genuine smile.

Shoot with an iPad

1 Launch the Camera app on your iPad and make sure the slider on the bottom right of the screen is set to camera, not movie. Aim your iPad's camera at your subject and then tap on the area of your screen that you want to be the focal point of your image, to set it.

2 When you're ready to take your shot, press the on-screen camera button, your image will then be stored in your iPad's camera roll.

Add fun effects with Photobooth

3 Don't forget your iPad is equipped with a front-facing camera too. To make use of it, tap on the reverse camera icon at the bottom right of the screen. You should now be able to see yourself and take a picture in the same way as step 3.

Launch the Photo Booth and you'll see the home screen, divided into nine squares, showcasing all the different effects the app offers. Choose the effect you like by pressing the appropriate square. When you're happy, tap on the camera button on the bottom of the interface to take your shot and then view in your iPad's Camera Roll.

:REMOTE SHOOTING

This is one for the true Apple devotee in that it requires two devices based on the iOS operating system, meaning an iPad, plus an iPhone or iPod Touch. Both devices need a copy of Camera for iPad, but you'll only need to pay for the app once as it's universal and will work on iPhone, iPod Touch, and iPad. The two apps can then communicate either over Wi-Fi, if both are connected to the same network, or Bluetooth. The application allows you to not only shoot the picture remotely, but to immediately transfer it to the other device. There is also a "flash" feature, which is admittedly of limited use. It sets the iPad's screen to bright white (or a color of your choice) at the moment of shooting so that, if it's positioned nearby, it can provide extra light to your subject. While the camera in the iPhone isn't exactly a professional tool, the one used in the latest iPhone provides better image quality over the original and would be perfectly acceptable for use while scouting locations if you don't have your camera handy. The Camera app for iPad and iPhone is relatively inexpensive, so some experimentation won't break the bank.

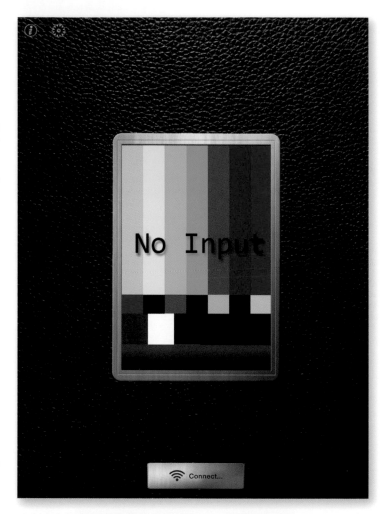

1 Launch the Camera for iPad application on your iPad, then launch the same app on your iPhone. You may see a message asking you to switch on Bluetooth, but this is not necessary if you are on a Wi-Fi network. Wait a few moments and the devices will find each other on the network, and you'll get smoother updates of your iPhone's current view.

2 Once connected you will see what your iPhone camera can see on both devices. Position your iPhone in the location you want to take a photo from, checking the iPad screen if necessary.

3 You can rotate the camera view on the iPad screen with a single-fingered rotary gesture to reflect the phone's orientation. You can also zoom in and out using the pinch gesture.

4 When you're ready, press the Take Photo button on the iPad to shoot your picture. Once you've finished, quit the app on both devices and return them to their respective home screens, as broadcasting images can be a battery-sapping process.

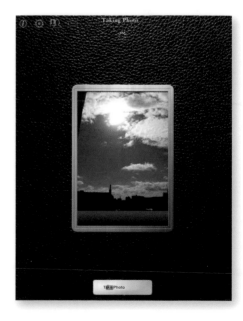

5 SHARING PHOTOS

Of all the iPad's skills, its most important is the way in which it displays photos. Why carry around a printed portfolio, when the iPad provides the photographer with access to a huge number of images and galleries that potential clients can interact with and enjoy using its impressive display? With up to 64GB of storage available, more images can be carried on the iPad than in a backbreaking number of physical albums, and the touch interface offers a far more intimate experience than viewing photos on a laptop or via a projector. The iPad offers a variety of ways to display images too, from simple image-by-image views that can be worked through by dragging a finger across the screen, to beautiful slideshows. Existing portfolios aren't ignored by the iPad either. It doesn't matter where you store your photographs online: you can access them on the iPad, whether they're part of a Flickr gallery or on your own website.

"the touch interface
offers a far more intimate experience"

DISPLAYING PHOTOS

Displaying photos on the iPad

The central source for images on your iPad is the Photos app, which offers a number of ways to view your images and helps to organize the photos in your library by date, location, and the people in them. The Photos app also provides the facility to create slideshows in a number of different styles as well as copy and email your pictures. When it comes to showing your images to clients, friends or family, this is the app you should go to. Every photo you've synced to your iPad or saved from the web or email is stored here and you can quickly interact with individual shots by swiping across them or pinching to zoom in and out. When showing a picture, the iPad is always aware of its positioning, so the photo will appear the right way up not just when you look at it, but when you flip the device over to let others have a look as well.

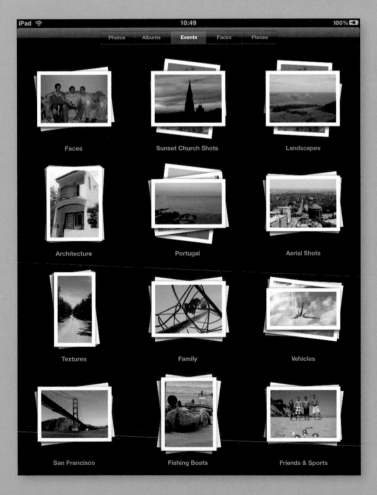

LEFT The iPad Photos app offers a number of useful ways to view your photos, while its intuitive design makes interacting with them a breeze.

65

:DISPLAYING PHOTOS

Photos

The iPad's default photo viewer is as simple as it gets, yet it's still a very effective way to show off photos. By selecting the Photos button at the top of the display, all of your images are shown as thumbnails which, when tapped, are displayed full screen. You can move back and forth between images with a swipe of your finger and zoom in and out by pinching two fingers on the screen. When a full-screen image is tapped on, a small bar appears at the bottom of the screen showing a preview of all the images on your iPad. You can run your finger along this display to quickly jump to a specific image in your collection. Should you have an Apple TV connected to your network, you can use the AirPlay button at the top of the screen to send your images to an HDTV.

Albums

The Albums view shows every album you have stored on your iPad and groups images into these collections. Tapping on an album will show all the images within it, but you can also pinch on a gallery name to peek inside it. The reverse is true once a gallery is open; by drawing your fingers together you can close the album and move back to the Albums view. Inside an album you can tap on images to view them full screen in the same way as the Photos view, and scroll up and down through the available images by sliding a finger up or down the screen.

Events

If you are using iPhoto or Aperture you can choose to organize your photos by Events. Events take the time and date from an image's metadata and group photos from the same day into an album. When you tap on the Events button at the top of the Photos app you will be shown a screen of all the available Events on your iPad. Tap on an Event to see the photos within it or pinch it open with two fingers to preview what's inside.

Faces

Faces is another iPhoto and Aperture-only feature that recognizes faces in your photos and groups them into albums of the same person. The actual recognition is done on the computer, and the photos are then tagged for use by the iPad. When you tap on the Faces button at the top of the Photos interface you will be presented with small polaroids and a representative picture of each person included in your collection of faces.

Places

If your images have been geotagged they can be displayed in the Places view on your iPad. Powered by Google, each different shooting location appears on the map as a red thumbtack which, when tapped, displays all photos taken at that spot. You can change the map view as you wish by pinching to zoom in and out, while you can also preview the images taken at a location by pinching on the image preview.

SLIDESHOWS

iPad photo slideshows

You can create slideshows for the iPad in a matter of seconds and still produce some attractive results. The option to include music and a variety of transitions adds to the effect and, should you have the requisite equipment, you can even send your slideshow to a larger display or projector when sharing photos with a larger audience. A slideshow can be created using all the photos on your iPad or pulled from a selected event or album. You can also select music from any song, playlist, or artist stored on your iPad as backing. In order to display the slideshow on a larger screen and the audio through speakers, you will need to have access to Apple's iPad Dock Connector to VGA Adapter or HDMI adapter, as well as a spare cable to run from the adapter to your display and an audio cable to run to your speakers should you be using the VGA option. Once connected to a TV, projector, or LCD computer screen, slideshows from the Photos app will be displayed on the screen. Audio can be output from the iPad's headphone socket via a mini-jack cable with a compatible connection at the other end for your TV or hi-fi system. Portable speakers will, in most cases, only require a mini-jack to mini-jack cable, which may be included or is readily available for little cost from most electronics stores. Slideshows can also be sent to an Apple TV connected to an HDTV using Apple's AirPlay technology to wirelessly stream the images. If you have the compatible kit and your iPad and Apple TV are on the same network, you can simply hit the AirPlay button on your iPad slideshow and select your TV from the pull-down menu.

Create a slideshow

1 Start by launching the Photos app from your iPad's home screen and selecting an Album, Event or all of your photos.

2 Now press the Slideshow button at the top of the interface to reveal the slideshow menu. Opt to turn music on by moving the slider to the On position.

3 Select a music track from your iPad's music library by tapping on the Music section and selecting something from the list of available tracks.

4 You can pick a transition from the list of available options just by tapping on its name. A check mark appears next to it. Start the slideshow by tapping the Start Slideshow button, and, if sharing the slideshow to a larger screen, make sure the VGA adapter is connected to your iPad and to the display.

SHARING A SLIDESHOW WITH AirPlay

If you're using Apple's iPad dock, you can give your office or meeting room a professional feel by showing off your portfolio while your iPad sleeps. When the iPad is locked and the Slide To Unlock slider is displayed, you can tap the Picture Frame button to launch a photo slideshow as a kind of screensaver that will display a selection of photos you choose. An added feature over the Slideshows in the Photos app is the ability to zoom in on faces found in photos as the images are loaded—ideal if you work with portraits or want to show off pictures of a specific person. The Picture Frame mode works perfectly when the iPad is sitting in its dock or held upright with a case. Leave it standing on your desk and you can show off your skills before you even begin your pitch.

1 First make sure your iPad and Apple TV are on and connected to your wireless network. Now set up your slideshow in the normal way.

2 With your slideshow ready, tap on the AirPlay button which should appear at the top right of the screen. Select your Apple TV from the list.

3 Tap on the Slideshow button and then tap on Start Slideshow to begin playing it on your Apple TV.

4 With your Apple TV selected on the AirPlay menu you can also flick through individual images which will be shown on your Apple TV.

A PICTURE FRAME

Use your iPad as a picture frame

1 Head to the Settings app from your iPad's home screen and tap on the Picture Frame option.

2 Set the transition you wish to use to anything from Dissolve to Origami by tapping on one of the options at the top of the screen.

3 Set Zoom in on Faces and Shuffle on or off to determine whether the iPad focuses on any faces it finds in your images and if it follows a linear order or mixes up your photos as they are displayed.

4 Select which photos you want displayed within the Picture Frame slideshow by tapping either All Photos (to display every picture on your iPad), or Albums, Faces, or Events to select images from a specific collection.

A PICTURE FRAME

Use your iPad as a Picture Frame

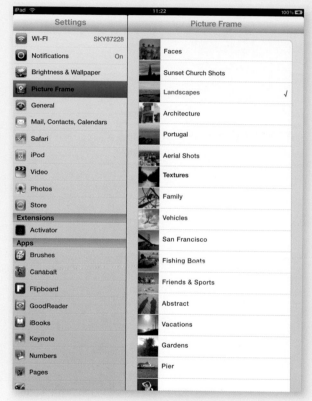

5 You can also choose which library the Picture Frame selects images from by selecting Saved Photos or Photo Library.

6 To launch your Picture Frame slideshow, lock the iPad using the Sleep/Wake button and then press the Home button to display the lock screen. Now click on the Picture Frame button next to the slider.

EMAILING PHOTOS

Sharing photos through email

One of the quickest ways to get your pictures to others is by sending them in an email. While there is a limit on the size of the email you send, you can normally fit a few snaps into a message and send them relatively quickly. It appears that the iPad automatically limits the email sharing to around five images so you may have to send your images across a number of emails if you want to share more. The process is best performed using a Wi-Fi network rather than 3G to improve transfer speed and reduce data use but either connection method will work fine. Images can be sent directly from your iPad's Photos app or copied and pasted into a new email message on the iPad.

Email photos from an iPad

4 Once you have selected all of your images hit the Email button at the top left of the screen to start composing a new email message.

5 Add your recipients, a subject, and some text to your message, and hit the Send button to share your pictures.

1 Start by launching the Photos app and viewing the Album or Event you want to pick images from. Alternatively, just show all the photos on your iPad.

2 Tap the Share button at the top right of the interface to begin selecting the images you want to send in an email.

3 To select an image or a group of images, tap on each one so that a blue circle with a check appears to denote that the image is selected.

6 SHARING TOOLS

For a while now, both the iPhone and iPad have included a feature called AirPrint that allows you to print directly from your iPad to a compatible wireless printer. This is by far the easiest way to print images from your iPad, and, if you have the right kit, is the best option. Should you not have a wireless printer, or for some reason don't want to update your iPad software, it is possible to export images from the iPad and onto a computer ready for printing. Should you wish to print directly from the iPad, Air Sharing HD, which we covered in chapter two, also provides a wireless printing option for Mac computers that will allow you to send images to a printer on your local network. This option may come in handy when you don't have a laptop or desktop computer with you but can connect to a Wi-Fi network that includes a shared printer, whether in an Internet café or as a guest on a friend's or client's network.

"it is possible to export images from the iPad and onto a computer ready for printing"

Printing wirelessly

There are a number of apps that offer wireless printing from an iPad and some are geared to specific printers. However, Air Sharing HD allows you to connect to all your available printers and doesn't require additional software installed on your computer to do so. Air Sharing HD simply searches the available wireless network for printers and sends your image to it. Air Sharing HD can also print PDFs and other compatible documents if you need it to. At the moment, the app only supports printing for Mac computers, but there are alternatives available including ActivePrint, which provides printing over any available network when connected to a PC running compatible software. All you need for either of these apps to work is a wireless network for the iPad and computer to connect to and a printer connected to your computer. Besides a little initial setup to configure the sharing of information between iPad, computer, and printer, all should be relatively simple.

Air Sharing HD

PRINTING WITH AIR SHARING HD

Print a photo from your iPad with Air Sharing HD

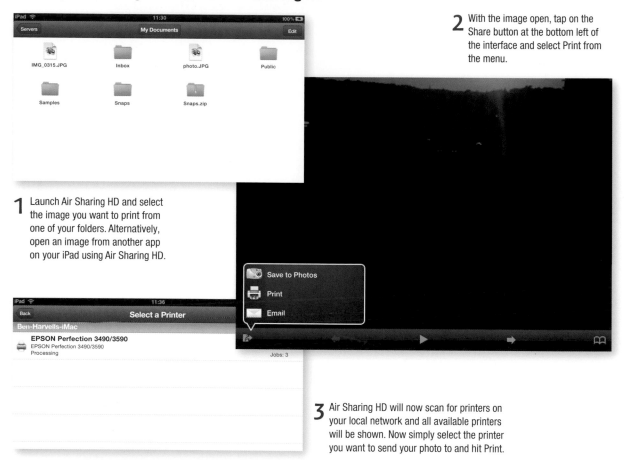

2 With the image open, tap on the Share button at the bottom left of the interface and select Print from the menu.

1 Launch Air Sharing HD and select the image you want to print from one of your folders. Alternatively, open an image from another app on your iPad using Air Sharing HD.

3 Air Sharing HD will now scan for printers on your local network and all available printers will be shown. Now simply select the printer you want to send your photo to and hit Print.

Print photos with AirPrint

1 Start by making sure your printer is switched on and connected to the same network as your iPad.

2 Now locate the image or document you want to print from your iPad's Camera Roll or Photo Library. This also includes emails and other compatible applications.

3 Tap on the Share button and select Print from the menu that appears. Your iPad will now list available printers and you can select which to use by tapping next to the word Printer on the Printer Options menu.

4 Select the number of copies you would like to print and tap on the Print button to send your image to the printer.

PRINTING WITH ACTIVEPRINT

Print a photo from your iPad with ActivePrint

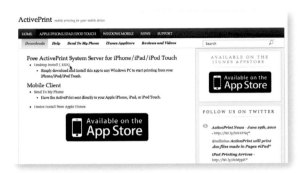

1 Start by downloading the ActivePrint Desktop software from iphone.activeprint.net, and set it up according to the instructions provided.

2 Now launch the ActivePrint app on your iPad and pick an image from your photo library to print.

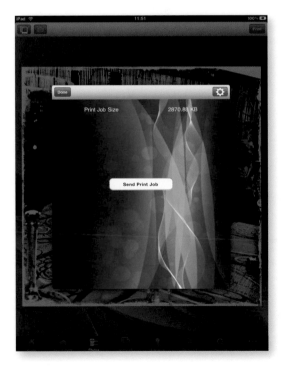

3 Position the image as you wish on the screen and then tap the Print button.

4 On the next screen enter your system address details and port number from the desktop software if you haven't already and give your document a name. Finally, tap on Send Print Job to print your image from your computer.

PORTFOLIO TO GO FOR FLICKR

Using Portfolio To Go for Flickr

Portfolio To Go is the perfect app for artists and photographers who use flickr.com to showcase their photographs online. Its elegant and intuitive Photo Wall gives users instant access to all of their Flickr photosets: you scroll each gallery horizontally to browse through the thumbnails, or scroll vertically to traverse through all the synced galleries. The main purpose of Portfolio To Go is to enable photographers to present their portfolio offline to clients. It's perfect for use with iPad Wi-Fi—just sync and go. Create and edit your photosets on flickr.com and Portfolio To Go will act as a presentation tool, keeping in sync with all your Flickr changes.

Portfolio To Go supports all iPad rotations, meaning it can be flipped vertically for portraits and horizontally for landscapes. Another unique selling point of this app is the "Send Portfolio to a Client" feature. The user carefully selects which of their galleries to share and can then send an auto-generated email to clients and friends containing a free download link to the "Portfolio To Go Player" iPad App. By clicking the emailed link, clients can launch and review the photographer's portfolio on their own iPad.

Sync and share your portfolio with Portfolio To Go for Flickr

1 When Portfolio to Go first launches it displays a Flickr login screen and then requests access to your Flickr account. It requests read-only access to download and cache both your public and private photos and photosets.

2 After logging into Flickr, Portfolio To Go starts downloading your Flickr photosets and creates local, synchronized, cached galleries on your iPad.

Portfolio To Go
For Flickr

3 Once your Flickr photosets
have been created locally,
Portfolio To Go automatically
loops through all of your
Flickr photos, downloading
and caching each photo in
turn. The speed of this process
is dependent on the size of
your Flickr photos and their
quantity, but you can check
the caching status by pressing
the spinning activity indicator.
Once this process completes
you'll be able to demo your
portfolio offline.

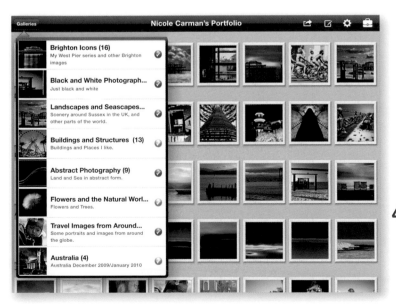

4 Each gallery can be scrolled
horizontally and the whole Photo
Wall scrolls vertically through
your Flickr photosets. Galleries
can be switched on and off
through the Galleries button
on the Photo Wall.

PORTFOLIO TO GO FOR FLICKR

Sync and share your portfolio with Portfolio To Go for Flickr

5 Touching any thumbnail will trigger the app to transition from the photo wall into a touch-responsive slideshow of the chosen gallery. Tapping the main image in slideshow mode makes the image go full screen.

6 Portfolio To Go enables you to send your selected Flickr photosets to clients and friends by email. Before using this feature, first select the galleries you do/don't wish to share (as in step 4). Next, use the settings pop-up to select the best image scaling option for your photos. Via the action menu you'll find the first option "Send Portfolio to a Client" will automatically generate an email with a link to your portfolio. The generated email contains instructions of two simple steps for clients and friends to follow to view your portfolio through a free iPad app called "Portfolio To Go Player."

ABOVE The old MobileMe Control Panel. From left to right, showing Mail, Contacts, Calendar, Galleries, iDisk, and Find My iPhone.

From MobileMe to iCloud

If you were a subscriber to Apple's MobileMe, then you probably know that was phased out in 2012. Your email service will still be accessible via the new address www.icloud.com. iCloud will also be the new home of your online contact and calendar syncing service, with features like Contacts syncing with a desktop computer, iPad, or iPhone. This, like MobileMe, is updated using "push technology" so that new information is reflected instantly across all platforms.

Creating a MobileMe Gallery in iPhoto or Aperture is as simple as creating a new album and dragging photos into it. These can then be sent to Facebook, Flickr, or a MobileMe Gallery. Those not using a Mac can still make use of the feature by using the online interface at me.com, but won't be able to sync images from the desktop quite so easily.

Gallery features

As you can see, the Gallery as it existed in MobileMe has been removed. You can use the Photostream for the most recent 1000 pictures, but for something more like the Galleries, you may need to wait and see—log onto www.web-linked.com/ipad for the latest updates.

BELOW The new iCloud service screen looks similar to MobileMe, but new tools can be added here by developers.

RIGHT The icon to return to the main iCloud page is in the top-left of each section (the Mail service, for example).

7 VIEWABLE WEB PORTFOLIO

If you sit down with a client, do you want to pull out a laptop, a heavy and possibly ragged photo album, or a cutting-edge slice of portable technology? As we discussed earlier in the book, the iPad makes a great first impression to clients, whether you're checking your email and updating your calendar, or showing them your portfolio. Your website does the same job and it's likely that, during the course of your meeting, you'll refer potential clients to it. In this scenario, depending on the design of your site, the iPad might fall down.

"the iPad makes a great
first impression to clients"

As this chapter will explain, there are certain elements of a website, if not the entire site, that won't display in the iPad's Safari browser. Showing a mwebsite full of holes where your galleries should be is not the first impression you're after. It's also worth considering that, with astronomic iPad sales worldwide, prospective clients may use their own iPads to view your site.

The reasons for this problem as well as a selection of solutions are coming up but, be warned, they come with their costs, both in terms of time and money. I've tried to balance the options for every budget but prepare yourself to spend a weekend tweaking your web presence if you want to remain truly compatible.

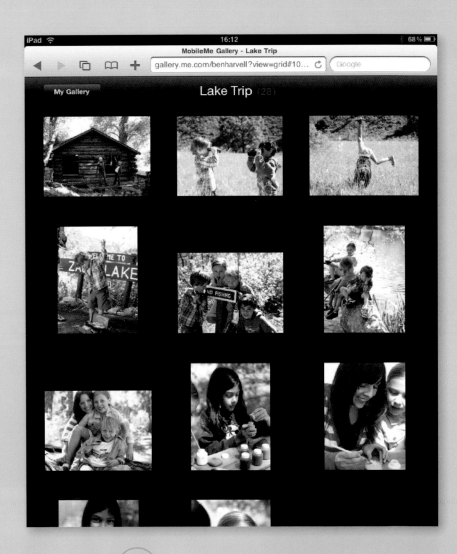

RIGHT A gallery is a guaranteed way to make sure your online images are compatible with iPhones and iPads.

FLASH ON THE iPAD

Flash and its lack of support on the iPad

One of the most complained-about iPad foibles is that it doesn't support Adobe Flash. If you don't know what Flash is, the chances are you should if you want your website to look good or even work at all on an iPad. Flash is a software language used to create anything from an entire website to games and web-based video players such as those you would find on YouTube.

It's not an accident that Flash won't work on an iPad either; it's a conscious decision made by Apple, who sees the technology as dated and full of bugs. Instead, Apple prefers the HTML5 standard. This may one day render Flash obsolete, but at the moment it's still in its infancy, hence a lack of widespread use. If you happen to browse to a web page that includes Flash content you will either be met with a message telling you to download the latest Flash software (which is impossible on an iPad) or even worse, an ugly blue block indicating the lack of Flash support.

As the popularity of the iPad continues to grow along with the iPhone and iPod touch (which also don't support Flash), most web designers and media outlets are catching on, providing their advertising, sites and video content in HTML5. But what about your site? If you have a self-made or professionally designed site made in the last five to ten years, the chances are it's filled with Flash elements, especially for the snazzy transitions and photo-zooming effects. In the worst case scenario, your site could have been built entirely in Flash making it completely useless on an iPad. So what do you do if this is the case? Fear not, there are options available.

Working around Flash

Whether you want to start again from scratch or employ a cheeky work-around, it's ultimately worth it. Not only will your site become instantly compatible with almost all modern mobile devices, you'll also be able to take your website with you wherever you go and show clients your pictures in a much more personal way. You ultimately have to ask yourself, will someone who visits your site on an iPad and sees nothing bother to launch their desktop browser to take a proper look? Take this step out of the equation and boost your compatibility and client roster in one move. And if, after all the options in this chapter, you feel like you may as well just start again from scratch, check out the information on Squarespace at the end of this chapter and later in the book.

Flash

BELOW Adobe and Apple have their differences when it comes to Flash and the iPad, but HTML5 is gaining popularity as an alternative.

The redirection method

Rather than have to go through the expense of completely redesigning your site or forking out for someone else to do it for you, consider this slightly fiddly method to send iPad users to a separate site that will be viewable on their device. If you make your own website using commercial software it's likely you know a little about HTML code and Java script. If not, and if you're using WYSIWYG (What You See Is What You Get) website design tools, bear with me—it's really not as terrifying as it sounds. The basics are this; every time a device with a web browser comes to your site, the site asks a variety of questions in order to decide what the device is, what browser it's using and so on. What you need to do is insert a tiny snippet of code that not only detects the iPad but also changes where the site takes that user.

To do this you will need to insert some JavaScript into the "header" section of your website's code to prevent the Flash version from loading and show something else instead. How detailed you want to get is your decision. You could create a separate version of your site with no Flash but then if you're going to go to that amount of trouble, you may as well just redesign your site completely. A simpler and more convenient technique is just to use the aforementioned code, which you can quickly find through checking in a search engine, to divert iPad users to a single page where you can link to essential information.

To do this you will need to create a separate page that holds this information and include links to your galleries and other web locations such as Twitter and Facebook. This can be easily done in most web design tools, while a skilled web designer will be able to knock this up within minutes. A simple message reading "Welcome to my site. You appear to be using an iPad. For the best experience you can view my portfolio here or contact me at this address." is all that is needed. Within this message you can include hyperlinks to your iPad-friendly portfolio and your contact information too. While this method isn't ideal, it does mean that those visiting your site with an iPad won't be completely left out and can still see your work in some form.

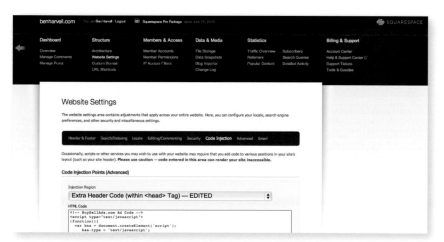

LEFT Injecting an iPad specific code into your website header is a simple process when using services like Squarespace.

FLASH ON THE iPAD

The redesign method

The overhaul route is time-consuming and potentially a little more expensive, but will certainly be worth it in the long run. It also means you don't have to worry about injecting code into your site because it will be instantly viewable on an iPad without having to redirect the user. First things first: rid your site of Flash. It's easy to spot Flash content on your website when using a desktop computer by simply right-clicking on an element and inspecting it with the Google Chrome™ browser. Even easier, load the site on your iPad and spot the sections that don't work. More often than not it's just a few simple elements like animated banners or adverts that merely make the site look bad rather than not function, but if you have a gallery built in Flash you're going to need to do a little more work. In many situations you can simply replace the gallery within your site with one that doesn't use Flash. There are many widgets and plug-ins available for free on the web that don't use Flash and can be embedded into your site quite simply or you could lay them out yourself on a single gallery page to show them off to your site visitors. In most senses, it's only the snazzy transitions of a Flash-based gallery that you will lose when creating an online portfolio, not the quality of the images themselves.

As technology marches on to newer, brighter horizons, your website shouldn't be left behind and, if your site was made more than five years ago, you should probably consider an upgrade anyway. Fortunately, as a part of the relentless drive toward more consumer-focused technology, web design is no longer a dark art that only those in the know can perform. Unlike the days when hideous tools like Yahoo Geocities were the only way for the casual user to design a page, today you can build a professional-looking site in minutes with no experience and for little cost.

Squarespace

One of the best services at the moment is provided by a company called Squarespace, which offers both hosting and site design in one affordable package. The service can be tried free for thirty days and allows you to be as involved as you wish in the design process. Offering a selection of ready-made templates and a What You See Is What You Get interface, Squarespace is the ideal place for a photographer without HTML chops to build a quality online gallery. Squarespace doesn't hide the more complex elements of a website from you if you want to get more involved either, so adding snippets of code to your site (as discussed in the previous section) is as simple as cut and paste.

Many photographers are already using Squarespace as a way to showcase their work and there's even an iPhone app (compatible with the iPad) that lets you update your site on the move. Being an up-to-date system, Squarespace will design a site that is compatible with modern browsers and this includes the iPad. While external widgets may include Flash elements, a Squarespace site, on the whole, will look just as good on Apple's tablet as it does on the desktop. If things really take off for your website, you don't have to worry about buying extra server space either. Squarespace simply ups your allocation as and when it's needed.

Padilicious

If you want to get a little more hands-on with your online portfolio and create a version of it that's not only compatible but designed for the iPad, padilicious.com is your best bet. This superb website is built to help Mac users turn a simple web page into an iPad-centric swipeable affair, and includes tutorials on how to create your own iPad web app, which can be hosted in the same way that you host a web page. All of the files you need are available to download from the site and there are handy tutorials as well as examples to set you on your way.

You don't need to be a design genius or have any understanding of coding to carry out the techniques either. All you need is a little patience and a few hours, and you can quickly make the most of this excellent resource. Once you have created your web app you can make it a stand-alone page on your site or incorporate iPad functionality right into your website for a truly seamless experience. This includes swipe functionality as well as orientation support so your pages look great in both landscape and portrait view on the iPad.

BELOW This brilliant site will show those with time on their hands how to make iPad-friendly elements for their website.

WELCOME TO PADILICIOUS.COM, a website whose only purpose is:

To provide easy-to-use Mac tools, that create browser-based content for display on computers and the iPad.

So browse this site, download and use the free tools, and tell your friends and classmates. Enjoy!

P-A • D-I • L-I • C-I • O-U-S • DOT-COM — PADILICIOUS!

HOW-TOs	TOOLS
VIEWING WEB-APPS ON THE IPAD Step-by-step instructions on how to enable a web-app to be displayed fullscreen on the iPad.	**CREATE SINGLE-PAGE WEB-APP** Create a single-page of scrollable text, optionally including an image, audio clip, or video, from text copied to the clipboard.
SHARING YOUR WEB-APP Step-by-step instructions on how to automatically deploy your iPad web-app to your MobileMe sites folder so it can be viewed by others.	**CREATE REAL ESTATE LISTING WEB-APP** Finally, and easy way for Real Estate professionals to create attractive interactive presentations of their listings.
ADD TOUCH-SWIPE SUPPORT TO PAGES Now you can easily enable web page elements to respond to single-finger swipes on the iPad.	**CREATE DIGITAL BOOKS** Automatically turn text files into digital books for reading in iBooks. Your publications can also include images, and audio and/or video clips!
ADD ORIENTATION SUPPORT TO PAGES Now you can make your webpages automatically adjust the page layout and design based on the way the user holds the iPad.	**CREATE MULTI-COLUMN ARTICLE** Create a multi-column article web-app using the currently selected text in any document. Additionally, the article can contain an image, audio, or video file.
BASIC IMAGE SLIDESHOW Step-by-step overview of how to create a basic image slideshow with dissolves as the transition between images.	**RENDER TEXT TO IMAGE** Adapt Keynote slides to work on iPad by rendering slide titles to images using non-default typefaces.

MAKING USE OF iWORK

Apple's iLife suite on the desktop has a counterpart in the productivity space called iWork. Essentially an Apple-only version of Microsoft Office, iWork provides a spreadsheet tool called Numbers, a page layout tool and word processor called Pages, and a presentation package called Keynote. These apps offer similar features to Excel, Word and Powerpoint and are also available on the iPad through the App Store.

While you will have to buy each app individually, it's Keynote that stands out as the major player for photographers, though the other two apps have their merits in certain areas and should be investigated.

"Keynote stands out as the major player for photographers"

Obviously, if you are already using a Mac, buying iWork is a sensible decision, as you can share your projects between your computer and iPad and take them on the road with you. You don't have to worry about compatibility issues if you choose to use iWork either. While Microsoft Office can't handle some of the more fancy tricks found in the iWork suite, the two play perfectly nicely together, with most Office documents readable in their corresponding iWork apps. In fact, when saving a document in Pages, Keynote, or Numbers, there is an option to save the file in common Office formats so you can send them to those using non-iWork apps. If there is anything included in your document that won't show up correctly in Office, the iWork app will tell you and suggest changes or make them for you. Since there is no version of Microsoft Office for the iPad right now it makes sense to use Apple's own tools. These not only provide all the features you need but also look the part as well. The three apps below come at a price, particularly if you buy all three, but when you consider the power on offer it's a price well worth paying.

RIGHT Apple's iWork.com is a handy tool when it comes to moving files between computers and users.

CREATING A CUSTOM PAGES DOCUMENT

If you're planning to share your work with others or simply need a fully featured word-processing tool on your iPad, you can't go far wrong with Pages. While many of the standard text editors on the iPad do a decent job of editing and storing text documents, Pages adds a layer of creativity allowing you to import images and adjust the layout of the page with simple strokes of your finger. There are also a number of default templates included with Pages on the iPad that allow you to add your own images. The templates range from letters to résumés and even projects, posters, invites, and proposals.

Created documents can be stored on the iPad or sent through email to Apple's iWork.com site or exported to another application. If you are using Pages on the desktop you can even send files to your iPad and work on them when you're away from your desk. As a photographer, the ability to access your portfolio when you're trying to create a letterhead or give a quick example of your photos is very useful. With

all the images you need already stored on your iPad, you can create a professional-looking Pages document ready to be sent out to clients without even needing to touch your computer. For larger projects, a connected Bluetooth keyboard would be ideal, such as Apple's own keyboard dock, but for smaller tasks the on-screen keyboard works just as well with Pages.

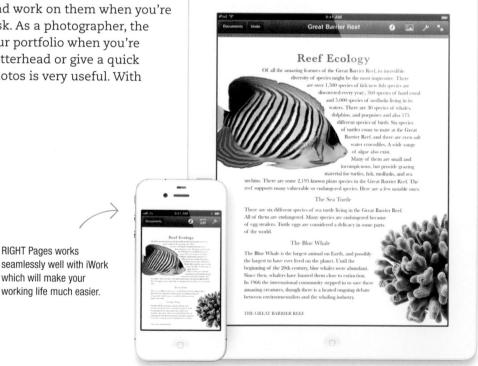

RIGHT Pages works seamlessly well with iWork which will make your working life much easier.

Create and share a custom Pages document

Pages

1 Start by launching Pages and tapping the plus button at the bottom of the interface. Now select New Document from the menu that appears.

2 Pick a template from the selection available, choosing whichever one seems most related to the document you want to create. You can also choose a blank template and work from scratch.

CREATING A CUSTOM PAGES DOCUMENT

Create and share a custom Pages document

3 Any image included in the document can be swapped for one of your own. Do this by tapping on the image button at the bottom right of the image and selecting the picture you want to add from your albums.

4 Any dummy text in the document can be selected, deleted and rewritten as you wish using the on-screen keyboard. You can also copy and paste text into the document.

5 When you're done, tap the My Documents button to take you back to the main screen, then tap the Share button to send your document by email, upload it to iWork.com or export it to another app.

CREATING A CHECKLIST USING NUMBERS

Just because you're working with figures doesn't mean you can't show off some of your creative skills while you do it. Numbers is Apple's iPad spreadsheet application, and it can do wonders for your bookkeeping whether you're in the office or out on a shoot. And it's not just a tool for budgeting with either. The app allows you to create all sorts of forms, charts and statistics and is an easy way to log data ready for use in iWork on the desktop or on your iPad when you have a spare few minutes. One very useful feature of Numbers is the ability to create a travel planner so you can cost shooting trips for clients and include travel and other expenses within the document. The output is truly impressive, with images and tables all available within the touch interface to make things look a lot more interesting than your standard spreadsheet.

As with all the iWork applications for the iPad, there are a number of preset templates to work with, so you don't have to start a project from scratch each time you launch the app. It's not all fancy design either; some serious calculations can be performed in Numbers, which uses an intelligent keyboard designed for entering dates, text, and numbers. The app is fully capable of creating and calculating formulas in the same way as a desktop spreadsheet tool. For costing a shoot or logging expenses this is an ideal application that, while not creativity-focused, could be an excellent aid to the working photographer.

1 Start by launching Numbers and tapping the plus button at the bottom of the screen to load a new spreadsheet.

Numbers

2 Select a new Checklist template from the menu that appears by tapping on it.

CREATING A CHECKLIST USING NUMBERS

Create a shoot checklist using Numbers for iPad

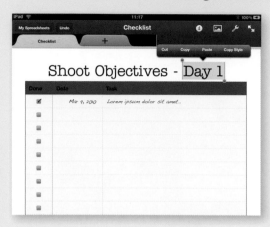

3 A new blank checklist will now be loaded. Tap on any areas of dummy text to add your own information using the keyboard.

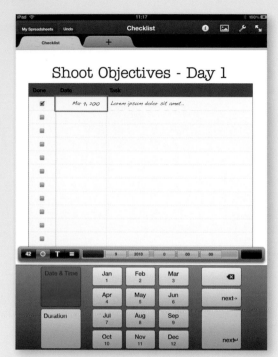

4 When you tap on the Date field a custom keyboard will appear allowing you to quickly add date information by specifying the day, month, and year using the display above the keyboard.

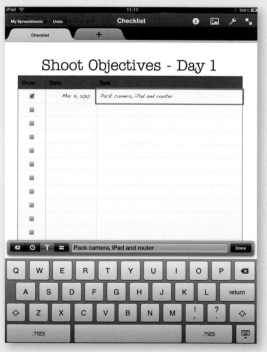

5 Enter text into the Task field to cover the various tasks involved in the current project, then repeat the process for all other tasks in your checklist.

6 If you need to add another checklist or include more Tasks you can create a new one by tapping the tab with a plus symbol on it and select New Form.

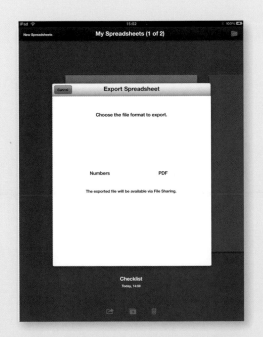

7 To share your checklist with others, tap the My Documents button and then tap the Share button to bring up the sharing menu.

8 If you want to share your checklist as a PDF or send it for desktop use you can choose Export from the share menu to include it as part of iTunes' file-sharing configuration.

CREATING A SLIDESHOW WITH KEYNOTE

Keynote

The big draw for photographers when it comes to the iWork apps for iPad is Keynote. Keynote is a presentation creation tool—the same tool that Apple CEO Steve Jobs uses during his presentations. The iPad version has been completely rebuilt for the iPad, and in doing so it becomes the ultimate in portable slideshow creation tools. While you can add text and charts to your project, a photographer is likely to want to use Keynote on the iPad solely as a slideshow creator and it's as easy as pie to do just that. With simple touch screen controls and access to your entire photo library, you can quickly build a slideshow that includes music, animation, and some gorgeous transitions that can be triggered by touch or set to run automatically. You can hand your iPad to a client and wow them with your exceptional slideshow.

Every image you add to a slideshow can include a different transition and you can add stylish effects to each slide including reflections, shadows, and frames. You control the timing of each slide too, by setting a delay time between each so you can linger on a particularly beautiful image a little longer if need be. The choice is yours. A clever little feature called Magic Move makes the creation of a dynamic slideshow even easier by automatically creating an animation based on two slides you have created. This could mean that one photo blends into another or that an image shifts in position to allow another to take its place. There are literally endless possibilities within Keynote to show off your photos in style.

You can even connect your iPad to a larger display or a projector using the Apple VGA connector and share the show with an audience. Slideshows can be exported as a PDF document or stored and shared by email in the Keynote format ready to be viewed on compatible computers or iPads. If you're using the Keynote desktop software you can even export your entire slideshow as a movie to be viewed on a wide range of devices, or uploaded to your website or YouTube. As well as creating slideshows, Keynote provides a dynamic way to pitch for new business—using your iPad as a key selling tool—or give talks to others regarding your photography. As with the rest of the iWork apps on the iPad, Keynote comes with built-in templates that you can add your own images and text to, or you can build your own designs from scratch. For those worried about mistakes, the Keynote undo button is neatly positioned at the top of the interface and will even work after you've closed and reopened a document. The fact that such impressive slideshows can be created so quickly is a bonus in itself, but the ability to do so wherever you might be with your iPad makes the app even more essential to photographers.

LEFT Keynote isn't just for business presentations. It also allows you to make impressive custom slideshows on your iPad.

96

Create a photo slideshow with Keynote

Keynote

2 Pick a theme from the available templates by tapping on it. For slideshows, a larger, cleaner template usually works best.

1 Launch Keynote from your iPad's home screen and tap on the plus button. Now select New Presentation from the menu to begin.

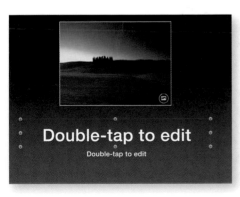

3 Tap on the dummy text and enter your own title text using the software keyboard. You can also move the text box if you want by tapping and dragging it.

CREATING A SLIDESHOW WITH KEYNOTE

Create a photo slideshow with Keynote

5 Now it's time to add a new slide to show off another picture. Tap on the plus button at the bottom left of the interface and pick a style.

4 Tap the button at the bottom right of the image in your template and select a cover image from your iPad's photo library.

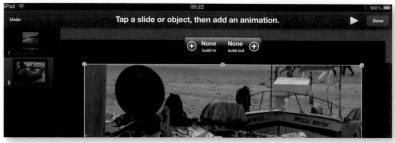

6 Add a new image in the same way you did in step 4 and then tap the Transition button, third from the right at the top of the interface.

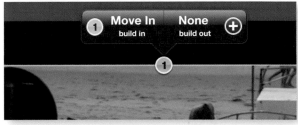

8 Tap Done and then select a Build Out effect in the same way. Repeat steps 4 to 8 until you have added all the photos you want to display and added effects to each.

7 Now tap the Build In button to choose the effect you wish to apply to your image as it appears. Tapping on an effect will preview it on-screen.

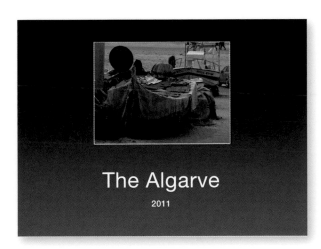

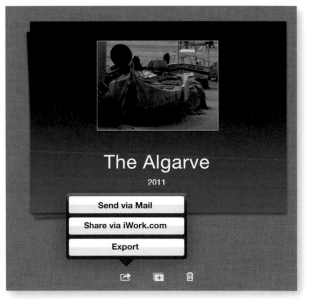

9 You can preview your slideshow at any time by tapping the play button at the top right of the interface. Make any changes you wish and then tap My Documents to return to the main screen.

10 You can now share your slideshow through email or iWork.com, or export it to another format or application by tapping the Share button.

iPAD & APPLE TV

Apple TV is aimed at the consumer market, allowing users to rent and view movies and TV shows on their HDTV. When combined with the iPad it's the ultimate entertainment tool, working on a wireless network to stream content from the Internet or Macs and PCs in the house. Apple TV can be controlled from the iPad using the Remote app or a new system called AirPlay, which sends media from the iPad to the Apple TV with a single tap.

This is all very impressive, but how does it impact a professional photographer? Well, it's the Apple TV's ability to play slideshows that's the major factor here; for less than the cost of a cheap compact camera, you can add this device to your office or waiting area and wirelessly show off your images on an HDTV as part of a client presentation. Any slideshow available on your computer or iPad can be accessed through Apple TV, and you can choose the soundtrack

"Apple TV, when combined
with the iPad, is the ultimate
entertainment tool'

from your iTunes library too. If you've exported slideshows as HD movies you can even choose to stream them through the Apple TV, playing them on the big screen while controlling playback from your iPad. What's more, Apple TV can be used to access MobileMe and Flickr accounts online, so you can quickly call up a specific album and share it with everyone from the comfort of your desk or living room. The device offers an HDMI port to send the video and audio signals to your TV and is small enough to fit in the palm of your hand. It also does a great job of streaming movies and TV shows if you have a little downtime in the studio. If you've been looking for a way to include an HDTV on your list of expenses for the year, the Apple TV might just provide the justification.

There are, however, a number of alternatives to the Apple TV that may suit you better and cost you a little less. The easiest one is to connect your iPad directly to your TV and show slideshows and movies you have created on the big screen, directly from the iPad. This technique requires the Apple Dock Connector to VGA or HDMI Adapter, but it does have limitations.

Having to keep your iPad plugged in to a TV the entire time isn't ideal, as you'll inevitably need to use it and the method does rather limit its portability. Instead, why not consider a second display for your desktop? For a very small price you can add a new monitor to your setup, which is worthwhile for storing palettes when editing photos on your computer anyway. When you want to show photos, simply attach your iPad and spin the display around. Of course, when in such close proximity to your computer this may seem a little frivolous, but you can take the monitor wherever you happen to be—in another room or on another desk.

RIGHT The Apple TV is more than just a tool for watching movies. It's also ideal for photographers looking to show off images and slideshows on the big screen.

CONTROLLING YOUR COMPUTER

Control your computer with an iPad

Another approach is to simply use your iPad as a control device for a computer connected to a monitor. Whether it's a laptop or desktop machine, wirelessly controlling your slideshow from across the room using an iPad will be just as impressive to clients. There are many apps on the App Store that will allow you to use the iPad as a large trackpad, including TouchPad by Edovia Inc. This inexpensive and useful app uses Wi-Fi to turn your iPad into the ultimate in remote controls.

Not only can you drag your finger across the screen to move the cursor, but you can also use the keyboard. The app can be launched quickly from the home screen and dismissed just as fast, enabling you to quickly switch to a specific photo in your slideshow and give clients a closer look on the iPad screen. If you're using TouchPad in low light you can also select a darker theme so that the iPad's display doesn't distract from your presentation. TouchPad supports multiple finger gestures too, so you can scroll and drag as you would on a laptop trackpad or with a mouse. Mac users get even more features, including support for Apple's Front Row media center software plus Exposé and screen zoom, which can be performed with a simple pinch of two fingers. It's perfect for looking at images in more detail.

Another app for controlling your iPad is iTeleport, which actually displays your computer's screen on your iPad so you don't even need to be anywhere near your office in order to access all your files and software. There are two versions of iTeleport available, one for accessing your computer on your local network and a more expensive version that allows you access from anywhere in the world provided you have an Internet connection. Both versions have their merits, the local version for avoiding unnecessary trips back and forth from office to studio, and the other could prove to be a lifesaver if you happen to leave photos and other files on your computer while on location.

RIGHT Control your Mac or PC from your iPad with TouchPad or iTeleport. The ultimate in remote control.

Touchpad

Use TouchPad to control your Mac with an iPad

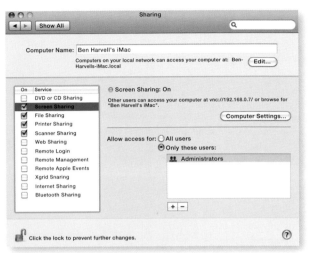

1 Start by downloading and installing TouchPad on your iPad then open System Preferences on your Mac.

2 Next, click on the Sharing button and then check the box labeled Screen Sharing.

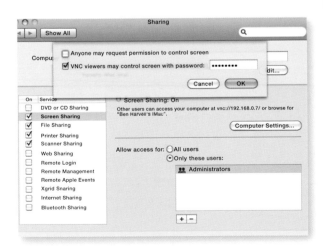

3 Now click on the Computer Settings button and check the checkbox at the bottom. Provide a password to use when connecting TouchPad.

4 Click OK and launch TouchPad on your iPad. Make sure your computer and Mac are on the same network and enter your password when prompted.

CONTROLLING YOUR COMPUTER

Use TouchPad to control your PC with an iPad

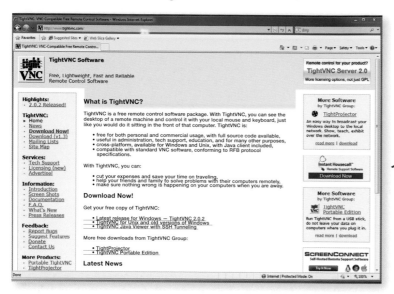

1 Start by downloading and installing TouchPad on your iPad. Now download TightVNC from www. tightvnc.com. Install and launch TightVNC once it has been downloaded.

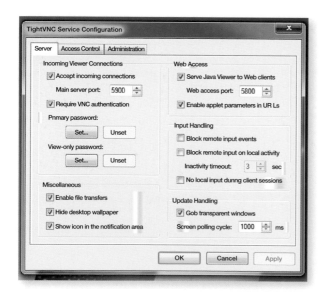

2 Find the TightVNC icon in the System Tray at the bottom right of the screen. Double-click on it to open the settings window.

3 Make a note of the port number displayed and set a new password. Now click OK.

4 Move your cursor over the TightVNC icon in the System Tray until a box containing your computer's IP address appears. Write the address down and launch TouchPad on your iPad.

5 Manually enter the server information using the port, password and IP address you have written down to connect to and control your PC.

Control your computer and share screens with iTeleport for iPad

1 Start by downloading the iTeleport app for your iPad as well as the desktop software available at www.iteleportmobile. com and make sure both your iPad and computer are on the same network.

2 Install the desktop software and enter your Gmail™ webmail service ID and password. If you don't have a Gmail account, you can create one at google.com.

3 Now launch the app on your iPad and follow the setup instructions. Once done you will be able to select your computer from a list and view and control its screen from your iPad.

ESSENTIAL ACCESSORIES

While you've got to know a number of useful accessories already in this book, this is a complete list of iPad accessories, selected specifically with photographers in mind. All the products you see here will either add additional features or improve your workflow and day-to-day usage. We've selected items from Apple and third party retailers as the market is now vast and, as you'll see, there are some incredible accessories out there—from solar chargers to waterproof cases.

If you've just got yourself an iPad, or are just starting to get your head around the importance of accessories, we advise you take particular note of the protection options—after all the iPad is a stunning tablet, made from fifty-percent-glass and you don't want to feel you've always got to have kid gloves on when handling it. Every photographer will need to get a memory card reader immediately—the lack of integrated camera card slots is the only criticism we have from a photographic perspective. If you use both SD and CF cards, you'll love M.I.C's All-in-one Card Reader. Have fun compiling your shopping list!

"all the products we've selected
will either add additional features
or improve your workflow and
day-to-day usage"

A BRIEF NOTE ON MAKING MONEY...

Making money with an iPad

Part of the point of this book is to help you find ways of helping you save or make money using an iPad. Here, however, I want to talk about a more direct route, which some may appreciate and others may loathe. Whether you like it or not, there's a big market out there when it comes to stock photography, and a unique niche within that market is made up by iPad users. The iPad and its App Store is an awesome vehicle for the photographer to sell their photos through apps. Not all of us have the requisite skills to code and sell an iPad app, but there are plenty out there who do and will gladly partner with a content provider (you) to share the profit.

There are also plenty of existing applications that require photographic content that you could consider providing. One option you might explore, for example, is to offer background images for iPad users. Crop a nice shot to fit the iPad display in either orientation and you've got yourself a background. People won't necessarily pay a fee per image but if you sold a pack of iPad backgrounds on your site or by way of the App Store you could stand to make a nice little residual income for very little work, using images you may not have made any money from had you not experimented. If you want to get a little more serious about the iPad market you could even consider creating your own personal application to enhance your brand. Ideally free unless you need to recoup the development costs, an app that shows off your photography could become the ultimate calling card for the modern photographer. There are hundreds of photo apps on the App Store but, with a little marketing and the right developer, you could quickly build a unique presence that will keep you ahead of the game. You might even pick up clients who have seen your work firsthand and want to see more. It might sound ridiculous, but there's a very real and very hungry market out there for the right kind of applications and the right kind of content.

Just Mobile Slide is a truly innovative stand for your iPad.

IMPROVING DAY-TO-DAY iPAD USE

Apple iPad Smart Case
www.apple.com

Apple's iPad Smart Case is a brilliant bit of design—it covers and protects both the front and back of your tablet, while adding very little extra bulk and weight. With the cover on your iPad still has that sleek, light feel. Smart Case is available in six bright colors and made from durable polyurethane. The case folds easily into a stand for reading, typing and editing photos. It even does double duty as a keyboard stand—just fold it back to tilt iPad into a comfortable typing position. Open the case and your iPad automatically wakes up, close it and it'll sleep. It's not cheap, but buy one and you'll see it's worth the money and will withstand the test of time.

All-in-one Card Reader
www.micgadget.com

The only real criticism the iPad has faced from photographers is the lack of integrated camera card slots. Well, M.I.C bypasses this problem with it's new all-in-one card reader, which support iOS 5.1 on The New iPad and comes with both SD and CF Card slots packed within its slim profile. The card reader has even been tweaked to be able to overcome the Voltage Limit set by the iPad and so supports even 600X CF Cards and Class 10 / UHS-I SD Cards! A must for a professional photographer.

Just Mobile AluPen
www.just-mobile.eu

While there's no denying the iPad's touchscreen is anything short of brilliant, when you're editing photos you want a tool smaller and more precise than your fingers. This is when a stylus comes in and we like this chunky pencil-shaped number from Just Mobile. Sculpted from aluminum, with a soft rubber nib, the AluPen gives a very smooth user experience.

Zagg InvisibleSHIELD Screen Protector

www.zagg.com

When it comes to protecting your iPad from scratching you can't beat Zagg's InvisibleSHIELD screen protectors. For photographers we recommend you choose the Hi-Definition shield that offers advanced clarity and a glass like finish—you won't notice it's there. Zagg's screen protectors are made from Military grade patented material and your purchase includes free lifetime replacement warranty for the life of your iPad, making it a very good investment indeed. If you don't want to use your iPad in a case, consider upgrading to full coverage protection.

Apple Wireless Keyboard

www.apple.com

If you're planning to use your iPad for emails, social media, blogging, your account or anything which requires a fair bit of typing you may want to get yourself a keyboard to use with your tablet. You won't find better than Apple's wireless keyboard, which uses Bluetooth technology to connect to your iPad, leaving you free to move the keyboard pretty well anywhere within range, and wirelessly type away. The keyboards sleek, slim, compact design takes up 24 per cent less space on your desktop than full-sized keyboards and features a low profile, anodized, aluminum enclosure with crisp, responsive keys.

IMPROVING DAY-TO-DAY iPAD USE

Just Mobile Slide

www.just-mobile.eu

If you use your iPad to show off your photos, either to clients or just in your home, you need an iPad stand that does it with style. The Slide is crafted from a single piece of high-grade aluminum. Thanks to the high-friction rubber cylinder stowed in its tubular support, you simply place the cylinder at the top of the Slide, lay your iPad on top and lift it to exactly the angle you need. The cylinder rolls down to hold your iPad firmly in place, in portrait or landscape mode and you have solid support for slideshows, editing and typing, at any angle.

ZAGGkeys PROplus

www.zagg.com

The ZAGGkeys PROplus is an ultra-thin Bluetooth keyboard, with doubles as a secure stand for your iPad and offers a comfortable typing experience. The PROplus model also has the benefit of backlit keys, in seven colors—great if you're a bit of a night owl and sometimes struggle to see the keys. The sleek design and high-quality aluminum means the 7mm thin keyboard matches the look of the iPad too.

Case Closed German Wool Felt Case

www.casecloseduk.com

When you use your iPad for client slide shows and meetings, you want it to look as stylish as your work. For this purpose we love the 3 mm thick, natural German wool felt sleeves by Case Closed. These are hand made in England from top quality soft materials. The sleeve is available in two sizes—with or without an Apple Smart Cover.

Power Traveller gorilla-pad connector

www.powertraveller.com

If these pages have inspired you to buy a minigorilla or powergorilla portable charger, this is the connector you need to connect these chargers to your iPad. The gorilla-pad connector features a resistor ID that converts the standard 5volts at 1amp USB into the 5volts at 2.1amps required by the iPad. It's a compact little connector weighing only 65grams.

Power Traveller solargorilla

www.powertraveller.com

Did someone say free power? Anywhere? Yep—up a mountain, or just on the move, the solargorilla portable solar charger gives your iPad and other electrical devises power. It works via two photovoltaic solar panels, which generate electric current when they are exposed to sunlight.

Power Traveller minigorilla

www.powertraveller.com

If you're likely to find yourself needing to charge your iPad when you're on a plane or in the middle of a field, then you'll appreciate minigorilla by Power Traveller. You can do a hell of a lot with an extra two hours charge! The tough and durable devise, with its laser-etched rubber coating features an LCD screen, which indicates battery capacity status and level of charge left in minigorilla, but the blue backlight will automatically turn off after five seconds to save power.

IMPROVING DAY-TO-DAY iPAD USE

The Ristretto for iPad

www.tombihn.com

Photographers who spend a lot of time out in the field with their iPad, or who travel frequently may find themselves in need of a bag for their tablet. The Ristretto, by Tom Bihn, is a vertical messenger bag with an interior, padded compartment sized specifically for iPad and designed to fit a few accouterments too—great for realizing that mobile office dream. Your iPad is protected in the built-in, interior, padded compartment, in the main compartment of the Ristretto. These bags are top quality, made with 6mm open-cell foam laminated with durable 4-ply Taslan on the outside and an interior of super soft-brushed tricot. The Ristretto has lots of clever features to make life easier including O-rings for keys and perhaps a Swiss Army knife for outdoors doors photographers. The included removable waist strap is a real bonus for travel and action photographers.

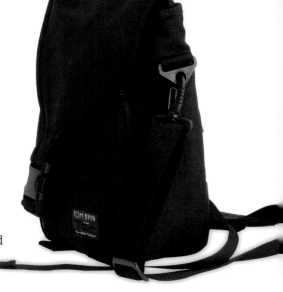

Apple Lightning-to-SD Card Camera Reader

www.apple.com,

If your camera uses SD cards, you can uses the Lightning to SD Card Camera Reader to transfer your images from your memory card to your iPad, via the Lightning connector. After you insert the SD card into the reader, your iPad automatically opens the Photos app, which lets you choose which photos and videos to import, then organizes them into albums. Handily, the Lightning to SD Card Camera Reader supports standard photo formats, including JPEG and RAW, along with SD and HD video formats, including H.264 and MPEG-4.

Incase Dual Car Charger

www.goincase.com

Whether you're on a photo tour of India, or simply not at home or in your office, sooner or later your iPad, like the rest of our power hungry electronics, will need charging. This car charger from Incase is so handy to have in your glove box—not only will it charge your iPad but you can also use if for other electronics you may have, your camera or iPhone for example.

Waterproof Case
www.ipadhut.co.uk, £27.95

If your photography means you'll be exposing your iPad to severe conditions, this waterproof case could provide you with the protection you need from water, sand, grit and mud. Although it's also a good buy for anyone who fancies editing images from the bath! Once sealed the waterproof case, made from flexible, crystal clear and UV-stabilized plastic, is airtight and becomes waterproof, keeping your tablet clean and dry, while still providing full surface access to the iPad's touch interface and keyboard.

Griffin Survivor Case
www.griffintechnology.com, $79.99

Tested and certified to meet or exceed US Department of Defense Standard 810F, Griffin's Survivor Military-Duty Case is designed from the inside out to protect your iPad. Get yourself one of these and dirt, sand, rain and a host of other environmental factors no longer pose a threat to your iPad. Survivor is built on a shatter-resistant polycarbonate frame clad in rugged, shock absorbing silicone. It's built-in screen protector seals the display from the outside environment, while hinged plugs seal the connector, camera, headphone port, hold switch and volume controls.

11 MUST-HAVE iPAD APPS

While we have already mentioned some great photography-related applications, there are thousands more to discover on the App Store. In this chapter you will find a handful of some of the best applications for the iPad: apps that will not only add exciting new features to your device but also those that help you interact with sites and services you may already use. Beyond that, there are also applications that, while not offering much in the way of workflow-enhancing power, will provide great inspiration to you as a photographer, which is crucial if you want to keep your work fresh and interesting. From tools to edit your images and organize them online, to apps that will help you engage with clients in unique ways, this section is all about showing you just what is out there when you scan through the photography category on the iTunes App Store. There are always duds, but the apps listed below are shining examples of the kind of quality that is also available. Best of all, some of them are completely free!

"from tools to edit your images
to apps that will help you to engage
with your clients in unique ways"

DISPLAYING PHOTOS

Bill Atkinson PhotoCard

Bill Atkinson is not only a professional nature photographer—he's also a great application developer, who has worked on Apple platforms to create such legendary programs as HyperCard, QuickDraw, and MacPaint. His PhotoCard app is an excellent example of a photography mind working in sync with the possibilities the iPad affords, and one that provides an impressive service to boot. Simply pick an image on your iPhone or iPad and you can send it directly from your device by email or regular mail as a professional-looking, high-quality postcard. Fun extra features allow you to add stickers and stamps and, if you're sending your card by email, you can even send a voice greeting to go along with it. This app is an excellent way to contact existing clients in a more engaging way, not to mention lure new customers.

Photocard

PHOTO-EDITING APPS

Masque

Masque is a well-thought-out tool that makes the most of the iPad's large screen and touch interface to allow the user to apply effects and perform image adjustments. You can pull images from a number of sources including Facebook, Flickr, or pictures in your iPad photo library, and make subtle or dramatic tweaks to your photos in seconds. Effects can be layered on top of one another, while advanced tools allow for gradients and brush adjustments to be painted onto an image with a finger, giving you complete control over the changes being made. Excellent for experimentation, Masque adds a new level of creativity to your photo editing on the iPad and allows you to share your work through email, Facebook or Flickr. A light version of the app is also available so you can try before you buy.

Masque

Tiltshift Generator

You might well write off this app as a gimmick but in truth it provides some unique tools to create some quite remarkable effects. Effectively faking the work of a DSLR, Tiltshift Generator makes it possible to adjust the depth of field of a shot to create spectacular visual illusions that even your camera might not be able to produce. The app offers a simple interface and some basic editing tools alongside the main controls. This is one of those apps that you won't use every day, but it offers an interesting way to manipulate your photos for specific project needs—or just for fun!

Tiltshift Generator

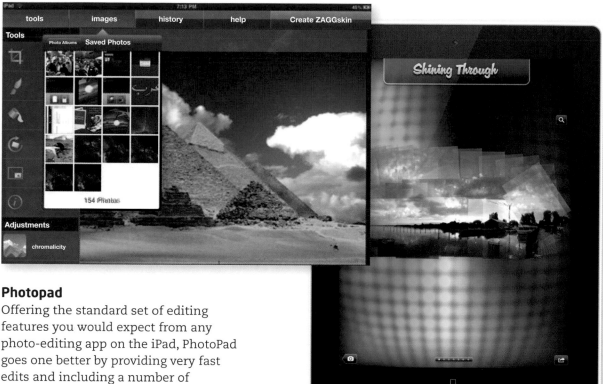

Photopad

Offering the standard set of editing features you would expect from any photo-editing app on the iPad, PhotoPad goes one better by providing very fast edits and including a number of interesting additional features. The app is updated regularly and offers a number of adjustment and positioning tools as well as effects. Made by ZAGG, a company that also makes iPad skins, you can design your own skin for your iPad within the app and order it from the website. It might be a little gimmicky, but think how this could work as a gift for your iPad-using clients...

Photopad

You Gotta See This

Originally for the iPhone 4, this app lets you create panoramic shots in a multitude of styles by simply sweeping your iPad's camera across a landscape, using the in-built gyroscope to piece individual shots into one image. While this won't produce professional-quality images, they can provide a fun addition to projects or as sample shots to showcase a proposed location. Saved images are stored to your iPad's Camera Roll and can be shared using any methods you already use, including email.

You Gotta See This

PHOTO-EDITING APPS

Photogene

The most fully featured iPad photo editor available, Photogene doesn't cost the earth and allows you to make simple or more complex edits on the fly—even when you're on location. The app was designed specifically for the iPad and makes good use of the available screen space providing red-eye correction, cropping, and color adjustments. You can transfer an image to your iPad during a shoot, make basic adjustments to the shot and fire it out by way of email within seconds. The app even works with Raw files and can store images to the iPad photo library or send them to Twitter, Facebook, and Flickr.

Photogene

Impression

Impression

Don't wait until you get back to your computer to watermark and share your images; do it on your iPad with Impression. Offering one and only one simple feature, this free app allows you to add text to an image as a watermark and then adjust the opacity and color to suit your requirements. If you want to share an image from the field but are worried about copyright infringement, this will be your go to iPad app from now on.

INSPIRATION & LEARNING APPS

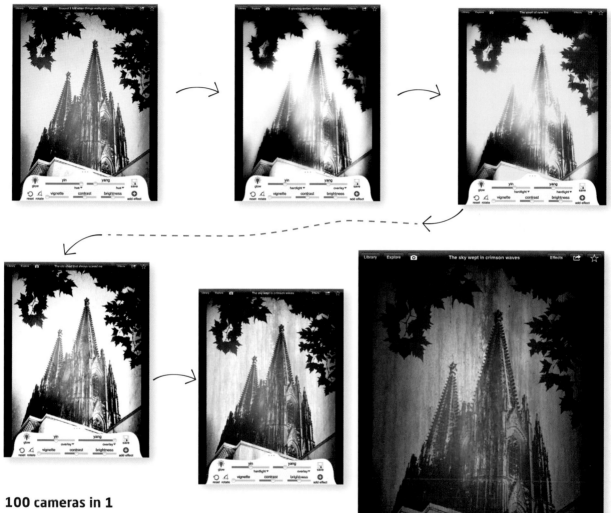

100 cameras in 1

A fantastically fun way to see how different photo effects look on your photos, full-screen, before tweaking the effect to suit your taste. You can pick any photo from your library, then just swipe left or right between the whimsically named effects ("The old shed that always scared me," for example). Once you've found one you like, tweak the sliders to change the "Yin," "Yang," brightness, contrast, or add a vignette.

100 cameras in 1

:INSPIRATION & LEARNING APPS

Guardian Eyewitness

Get a daily visual reflection of global events via striking and beautiful photographs from The Guardian. Access the last hundred images from the award-winning photography series, view images' EXIF data and read tips from the photographers themselves. Save images you love as favorites and share them via email, Twitter and Facebook.

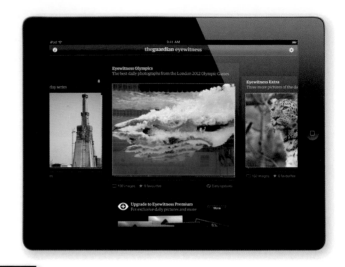

Explore Flickr

Need some inspiration? Make the most of flickr.com on your iPad with this great app that shows you stunning photography from around the world in high definition. Move between full size images by just sweeping or watch a rolling slideshow. Explore by Tag, search for keywords and keep track of your favorite searches with Search History.

Fotopedia Heritage

This brilliant app, created in cooperation with UNESCO World Heritage Centre, manages to bridge the gap between world photo book, inspiring travel guide and bedtime relaxation aid. Fotopedia Heritage does so much—instant slideshows, travel planning, and point of interest descriptions—you can even travel the world in photos by shaking your iPad to shuffle.

Stuck on Earth

Want to find the best places in the world to visit, photograph and experience. It's such a brilliant scouting tool that allows you to discover millions of amazing places to photograph. If you like to explore and travel you'll love this app—it's inspiration potential is endless and you can even create and save trips for the future!

50 Greatest Photographs of National Geographic

Get the behind-the-scenes stories about each of the fifty iconic images that make up the National Geographic's prime collection—from the photographers themselves. Watch videos explaining how the photographers got the shots and view the sequences of photographs that were taken in the field and find how the perfect shot happened.

The Wider Image

This impressive app, from Reuters—the world's largest news agency brings news photography to life. Look beyond the news headlines with the best stories from Reuters photographers worldwide, often with a human perspective. See what's happening in places you care about and discover stories in places you may never otherwise have got to know. You'll expand your news photography horizons in so many ways.

PLANNING & ORGANIZATIONAL APPS

Todo for iPad

Why take a real binder out on a shoot with you when you can have this virtual assistant stored on your iPad? Keeping track of your day-to-day or shoot-specific tasks has never been easier than it is with this beautifully designed app, which helps you plan and carry out activities using simple checklists and organizational tools. The app can sync back to your computer to keep you up to date at all times and it's fully compatible with the contacts and calendar apps on the iPad, ensuring that you can also send out information to others. You can even set alerts and prioritize events on your to-do list by order of importance if you wish. For keeping yourself organized with your iPad, Todo offers the right mix of form and function.

Todo for iPad

Simplenote

Don't scrabble around looking for paper and a pen each time you need to make a note, use Simplenote to not only jot down important info, but keep it all in one place and share it with others. All of your notes are synced back to the Simplenote website, so you can access them from anywhere and don't have to worry about losing your data either. The app is free to download and ideal for drafting emails, recording data or making lists.

Google Mobile App

Let your iPad help keep you organized. Google's Mobile App, available for both iPhone and iPad, allows you to search by voice and uses your current location as a reference. The app also allows you to quickly connect with other Google services such as Gmail, Google Calendar, Picasa, and Maps with a single tap, making it a one-stop shop for all your communication, navigation, and organizational tasks. Other search features include a contact search, Google Suggest, and you can even set the app to send you a push notification when you receive new emails or calendar events. If you use one or more of the Google services you need to install this free app on your iPad.

Simplenote

Google Mobile App

UTILITIES

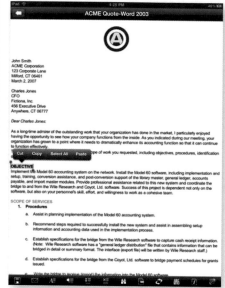

Wolfram|Alpha

How many times per day do you ask yourself questions like "How far is that in miles?" or "What's that in dollars?" Wolfram|Alpha can answer practically any question you can throw at it. Whether it's a simple conversion or calculation or a more complex geographical or historical query, the app does its best to read your input and formulate an answer based on its own knowledge and the power of the web. There are even built-in tools for photography too, including f-stop arithmetic, subject magnification, depth of field, hyper-focal distance, and more.

Wolfram|Alpha

Documents To Go

Think of this app as Microsoft Office for your iPad, enabling you to open any Word, Excel or Powerpoint file, as well as many others, from Apple's iWork. You can import and edit any document on the iPad using Documents To Go and then share it with others through email, or sync files back to your desktop to make sure they remain current. One of the major features that Documents To Go offers over other Office-like apps is its ability to work with sharing services like Dropbox. Simply connect to your account, work on the shared files and then save them back to your shared folder. Believe it or not, a large portion of this book was written using Documents To Go and Dropbox.

Documents To Go

iDisk

If you're still using Apple's MobileMe service you'll also be allocated a chunk of online storage known as your iDisk. You can copy files to this online storage space from your computer or by way of the web and access them on your iPad wherever you have an Internet connection using the iDisk app. Files are sorted into folders and, if you are sharing a public folder, you can transfer files to your iDisk for someone else to view and vice versa. Storing your essential files and images on an iDisk is the easiest way to access documents without taking up space on your iPad's hard drive. Be quick though, the service expires in 2012.

iDisk

UTILITIES

Thanks to the iPad's networking capabilities and Adobe's ingenius extensions to Photoshop, it's now possible for developers to create apps which let you use your iPad to control the photographer's most established tool, Photoshop. Adobe has led the way by creating some handy apps to get you going (and prove their point).

Nav for Photoshop

Putting the Photoshop Toolbox at the tips of your fingers, Nav for Photoshop creates a link with your computer over Wi-Fi and gives you quick and instant access to the main controls.

Nav for Photoshop

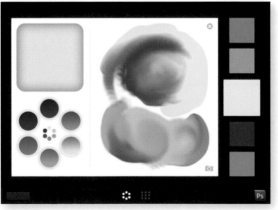

Eazel for Photoshop

Like watercoloring with your fingers, this app will let you play with color and see how it mixes. Tap all your fingers on the screen to bring up the options, and send the result to Photoshop.

Eazel for Photoshop

Color Lava for Photoshop

A color-mixing tool that replaces the classic Color-Mixer panel in Photoshop with a more natural approach that might appeal to those of a more painterly disposition.

Color Lava for Photoshop

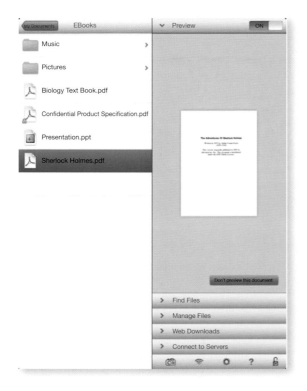

Goodreader

If you don't feel the need for a full office suite, you can keep your iPad compatible with most document formats with the reasonably priced app, Goodreader. The app is designed for viewing large PDF and TXT files, but it also handles a wide range of other document formats. Using a unique reflow technology, Goodreader extracts pure text from PDF documents and flows them onto the iPad's display with text wrapping and search features included.

Compatible with Apple's Dropbox and many other online services, you can access your files wherever you are within Goodreader and even open non-iPad-native mail attachments in the app.

Goodreader

Dropbox

Dropbox has been referred to a number of times in this book, and the reason is simple: it's an essential tool for keeping your files up to date on your iPad, as well as across all your computers. Simply create an account via the Dropbox website, install the software on all your computers, and your iPad and files will be available wherever you are. You can even edit files on one computer and see the changes reflected on all of your other devices. You will need an Internet connection in order to make use of Dropbox and ensure all your computers are connected to stay completely in sync. But once that's done, there's no other setup to perform. Many iPad apps are compatible with Dropbox syncing too. Best of all, the app is completely free and provides 2GB of storage.

Dropbox

PHOTO-SHARING APPS

Photobucket

If you're already a Photobucket user then you'll know that it's a useful online storage resource for photos and video, working in the same vein as Flickr. The Photobucket app offers a way to send images on your iPad to your Photobucket account and even caters for Geotagging and a host of other interesting features. Differing slightly from other online gallery-based apps, Photobucket for iPad also allows users to search and download any image from the site as well as share images through email. Albums can be edited and created from within the app and individual images can be named, renamed and deleted on the fly. For a free application, Photobucket offers a decent bunch of features—almost enough to make you think twice about your current service if you're not on Photobucket already.

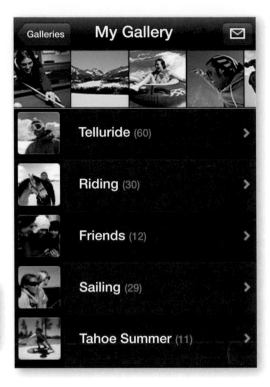

Photobucket

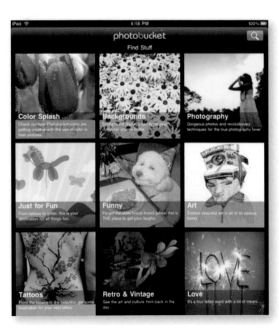

MobileMe Gallery

One app to definitely take advantage of is the free MobileMe Gallery app. Designed for the iPhone, it works fine when blown up to twice the size on an iPad and, while it won't provide the most incredible portfolio viewing experience in comparison to a native iPad app, it's still handy for quickly viewing your published albums and sharing them via email. The interface includes an attractive scrolling panel at the top of the display, which shows off a random selection of pictures. You can dip in and out of albums with a single tap.

MobileMe Gallery

Photo Slides

Another app for showing off your photos rather than manipulating them, this clever and inexpensive app connects to Flickr and displays a slideshow of images from the site. What makes Photo Slides exciting for the photographer however, is its ability to search for photos you've tagged on Flickr. You can set a slideshow of your most recent images or your entire gallery while your iPad isn't in use or when showing your work to others. The interface isn't beautiful but then you don't want fancy graphics distracting viewers from your photos now, do you?

Portfolio To Go for Flickr

This app is ideal if you want to take your photos with you wherever you have your iPad and an Internet connection. And even if you can't access the web, you can cache galleries for offline viewing, not to mention view all of your galleries using the Photo Wall, and send specific galleries to clients via email. You can also share images through Flickr links on Facebook and Twitter. The interface is easy to use, which is great news if you want to showcase photos to clients and let them flick through them for themselves. If your primary source of online photo storage is Flickr, this is one app you won't want to be without.

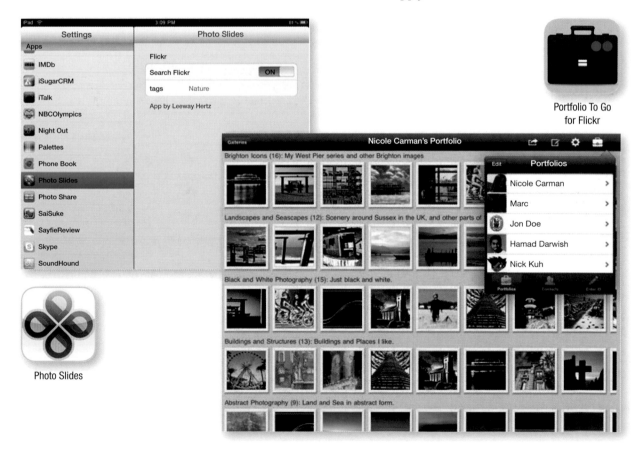

Portfolio To Go
for Flickr

Photo Slides

12
ESSENTIAL ONLINE SERVICES

As a photographer, you no doubt have favorite services that have served you well over the years. I certainly don't want to sway your loyalty or suggest change for the sake of it, but in this chapter you will find some iPad-centric services that will help you better use your device. In an increasingly online world, the ability to keep apps and services synced wherever you are, on your desktop computer, laptop and iPad is essential. By using services that are iPad-friendly you'll be helping yourself stay organized and reduce physical syncing times with updates to your files and folders happening over the air.

"by using services that are
iPad-friendly you'll be helping
yourself stay organized"

SERVICES FOR iPAD PHOTOGRAPHY

Photobucket

Photobucket merges social networking with image hosting to provide a unique way to share and link to your photos and videos. The service allows you to edit pictures on the site too and share them on sites like Facebook, Twitter and MySpace. With a free iPad app available, Photobucket is a great option for iPad users and provides an easy way to view your photos on your iPad when you're away from your desk.

Flickr

Flickr is quickly becoming the go-to image hosting service on the web, providing a wide range of images for a worldwide group of users sharing over four billion photos. The site is both clean and functional and there are a number of applications for the iPad that allow you to access your images on Flickr, including Portfolio To Go. Images can be shared, geotagged, and set with varying privacy controls and usage rights.

Photobucket

Flickr

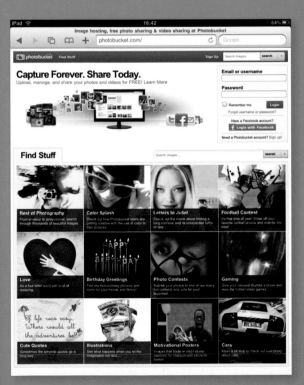

:SERVICES FOR iPAD PHOTOGRAPHY

Squarespace

iCloud

Squarespace

Squarespace.com is probably the best service for creating your own portfolio website. The site assumes no experience on the part of the user but allows you to delve into the code of your site if need be. Offering beautifully designed templates and photo gallery pages, you can create a professional-quality site in minutes without the cost of a web designer, and your site won't look templated or like any other. Squarespace offers a varied pricing structure and its servers adjust to the demand for your site. It should survive even if your work starts getting some serious attention.

Padilicious

Padilicious.com offers all the files and instruction you need to create iPad-oriented web applications that include swiping capabilities and more. The site is free to use and the support files free to download; the only thing you need to invest is the time to make your apps and add them to your website so that fellow iPad users or yourself can show off portfolio images in style. There is a selection of guides available on the site and more are added frequently, so check back often for the latest tips to enhance your online presence for iPad users.

iCloud

iCloud is the ultimate wireless storage service for iPad users, combining music, photos, apps, calendars, documents, and syncing across all of your computers and compatible devices. Taking over from Apple's MobileMe service, it integrates seamlessly into your apps, so you can access your own content on all your devices. It also comes free with iOS 5. The syncing tools mean that new info is "pushed" to your iPad, including email and calendar updates.

Photoshop.com

If you use any of Adobe's apps such as LightRoom or Photoshop or even the entire Creative Suite, you should investigate the features offered by photoshop.com for sharing and editing your images online. The corresponding Photoshop Express iPad app makes accessing and adjusting your images easy when you're away from your studio. If you're used to the Adobe layout, the website and app will also be very familiar to you and so easy to use.

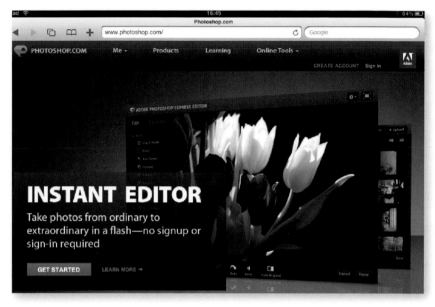

Photoshop Express   Viewbook

Viewbook

The guys at viewbook.com are well aware that photographers use the iPad in their work and, as such, have created a way to design professional portfolio websites, photo galleries and presentations that work seamlessly with your tablet. Images stored on Viewbook can be promoted and organized and you can even sell your images from the site. A free 30-day trial is available at viewbook.com so you can sample all the great features.

PROFESSIONAL PERSPECTIVE

Through the pages of this book you've seen how the iPad will change the way you work. There's nothing quite like hearing it from like-minded souls though, so over the next five pages you'll find words from top professional photographers, who talk about how they use the iPad and the effect it has on their workflow and business.

With the iPad being a truly multifunctional tool for photographers and its uses expanding daily, thanks to the abundance of new apps, it's really interesting to see how photographers from different genres, at the top of their game, use theirs. As you'll see, the iPad has dozens of uses for professionals, from showing clients all singing, all dancing slideshows of images to using it with Capture One in the studio for commercial shoots.

One thing is for sure, all of the photographers we spoke to in putting this book together, not just the ones on these pages, agree that the tablet has improved their work flow like no other technology to date. Be prepared to be inspired by the words of fellow photographers and feel excited about what you'll achieve with your iPad.

"The iPad is fast becoming the Swiss Army Knife in the professional photographer's kit bag'

KELLY WEECH

Contemporary Wedding Photographer
www.kellyweechphotography.com

"The iPad has given my business so much freedom that sometimes I wonder how I ever managed without one. I use my iPad in the day-to-day running of my business and it became an essential piece of kit from day one. It gets used for everything from regularly checking and responding to emails, showing my portfolio at the click of a button, presenting my images in an easy way to existing and potential clients, interacting on social networking sites with suppliers, researching online without waiting for my laptop to boot up—everything just seems to be so simple.

"The beauty of the iPad is that you can customize your iPad to suit your business. With so many apps on the market, the choice of solutions is endless—I've always been able to find an app perfectly suited to my business needs and requirements. Apple's App Store is constantly being updated with new and innovative ideas that make life and running a business easier in all aspects. My iPad saves me time, money and space by being a multifunctional tool.

"Everything from my accounts to portfolio, research and ideas to model release forms can all be available at the click of a button, anywhere in the world. When you work primarily on your own, juggling all the different aspects of a business can be overwhelming, especially when you spend days away from the office. These days I don't worry as much knowing that I have my iPad at hand at any given moment, containing everything I may need.

"Although I don't think the iPad will ever replace image editing on my laptop, I'll never say never. For now, I am more than happy to use the editing facilities I have on my iPad as a mock-up to show clients and for Facebook and twitter sharing.

"Lastly, I like that the iPad looks and feels like a portfolio which can easily be updated and sorted to present to a variety of clients. With its slick looks, functionality and great image display options, it is the ultimate solution and alternative to lugging around a number of albums and laptop—it's saved my back!"

ADAM GASSON

Freelance photographer
www.adamgasson.com

"For me, the iPad is fast becoming the Swiss Army Knife in the professional photographer's kit bag. In the studio, using it with the Capture Pilot app, it has become an incredibly valuable tool. For most studio work I'm shooting tethered to my MacBook Pro through Capture One and if the laptop is plugged in it can be a real time waster having to go back to check images after every shot—but with the iPad you can have live previews in seconds. The app quickly allows you to check critical aspects such as focusing, exposure and sharpness. It also works perfectly for shoots with creative directors or stylists, allowing them to see the shoot from anywhere in the studio, without having to huddle around a computer monitor. It's brilliant when you're working with a model as they can see how they look without having to break away from their pose.

"Away from the studio, the iPad is a perfect portfolio tool for taking out on the road. I can build up a large gallery of images and then tailor the portfolio to each client I'm going to see. The savings in printing cost is more than the cost of iPad alone! The high resolution screen presents images very well and the intuitive navigation creates a user-friendly viewing experience. In meetings the last thing I want is the art editor to lose focus on my work, so this last point is key. In addition to showcasing my work directly I can also use Newsstand to download latest editions of magazines I've worked on—and again the pages are crystal clear, much better than a wrinkled cut out page!"

PAUL TOEMAN

Event Photographer
www.paultoemanphotographers.com

"The iPad has literally revolutionized how I interact with my clients, present images and confirm new bookings. The flexibility to use it in a cafe with a potential client is so great—with two pairs of headphones plugged into the iPad and they can watch a musical slideshow of my best work and be swept away by my images! I can show the depth of my services and portfolio by accessing and showing my website online—including an in-depth discussion of how my pricing works—all using a hand-held devise with easy-to-see, beautiful screen with no wires needed!

"I also keep up to date with clients and prospects via emails, Facebook messages and twitter comments, as well as promoting my latest work, thoughts and initiatives through these social media tools. I can check my calendar and get straight back to an enquiry confirming my availability, as well as set up lead meetings.

"Finally, when I come to present a client's final edit I bring my iPad to their home, connect it to their flat-screen TV via an HDMI lead and allow them to view their event photographs on their own TV! In all the iPad makes me look professional, approachable, relaxed and contemporary."

BEVERLEY CORNWELL

Fine Art Photographer
www.burninglens.com

"I've been using the iPad for a couple of years now, in several different ways for my photography. It's a great tool for showcasing images and I always take it with me to meetings with galleries and clients. I keep my portfolio and a copy of all my artist statements on there, which means my work is immediately available to view and I don't have to worry about finding a Wi-Fi connection and then waiting for web pages to load. I can take notes in meetings on it and add any events to the calendar too.

"As the iPad starts up so quickly it saves the awkward moments that you sometimes get waiting for a laptop to boot up—you know the moments when you're hitting at the buttons and everyone is staring at the little timer spinning around... I can get straight into to talking about my work instead. Clients appear to like it because they have immediate access to the images they want to see and it's very hands on. We can scroll backwards and forwards discussing my photography and I feel like they really engage with my work though, thanks to the tablet. I also know that my videos will always run and play smoothly at high quality, plus my images will look exactly as I want them—there's nothing worse than opening up your portfolio on a badly calibrated monitor that's either too bright or too dark and has color casts affecting the tones you spent hours perfecting when creating your prints.

"I use the iPad to edit images too. These tend to be iPhone photos that I then upload straight to my blog. With the shared Photostream function you can access pictures really easily from the iPhone and the bigger screen makes it much easier to make fine adjustments. Snapseed is another of my favorites if I want to add filters that really change the tone of an image."

DAVID CLAPP

**Landscape and Travel Photographer /
Photographic Writer**
www.davidclapp.co.uk

"I have been using the iPad for almost 3 years now and I've never come across an IT tool that is so remarkably useful for my business. Initially, many photographers were being sold the iPad as a way of 'displaying their portfolio to potential clients,' but I could never see this as a reason to purchase one. I never actually meet clients face-to-face as this is something I can always do via email. I did initially believe that the iPad's potential was perhaps a little limited—how wrong I was.

"I went straight for the 64gb iPad 2 with 3G. Using phone networks for email and Internet was just the start of its potential. Goodbye expensive roaming tariffs for using my telephone abroad. On landing in a foreign country, I buy myself a 3G network card from the airport, costing no more than £5 for a week of connectivity. I then began to find myself sat on the steps of a church answering my emails, instead of taking time out of vital shooting time to hunt out McDonald's for free Wi-Fi. I will never forget missing a pre-iPad image sale of nearly £1500, all because I didn't check my emails regularly. This will thankfully never happen again.

"I began to find great uses for staying in contact with the UK. I could make 3G phone calls using the Skype app for just 1p a minute. I could keep in touch with my bookkeeper, avoiding any potential business problems and contact my friends and family back home, virtually cost free.

"Oh, but it doesn't stop there. There are apps that are vital for landscape and travel photography. Let's start with Google maps. Whilst driving in foreign countries, this essential app can download map data via 3G whilst on the move. The Photographers Ephemeris, an app that calculates sunrise / sunset moonrise / moonset anywhere on the planet, is a vital program that also needs Internet connectivity. Forget data roaming and other excessive phone network charges, a 3G Sim card will sort all this for the cost of two cappuccinos.

"What about data storage? I never use the iPad as a storage device as it's far too irritating, inhibited by Apple's rather strict operating system. It's this point that I find a laptop to really comes into its own. Finally, I still haven't found a reason to upgrade to an iPad 3 or iPad 4!"

A FINAL WORD

Filling this book with all the information you need to make the most of your iPad hasn't been hard—the tablet has so much functionality for photographers, I could probably have filled these pages twice. The iPad really is a great devise for photographers with so many uses, from showing clients beautiful slideshows of images to using it with Capture One in the studio for commercial shoots. It really does enhance the way we work, no matter our chosen genre. That coupled with

the fact it's a back saver: significantly cutting down the amount of gear you have to lug around when you're out on a shoot, makes it an essential bit of kit.

The iPad still isn't a perfect tool for photographers though—we'd all love integrated memory card slots, a better camera and bigger storage capacity, but it's important to remember that it is a consumer devise. However, it's constantly evolving through software, which

"where there's a need,
there's a developer creating an app"

gives it a real edge over other tablet devices on the market. Where there's a need, there's a developer creating an app and the photography app market has pretty much everything you could wish for already, from inspirational apps from the likes of the National Geographic, showing off some of the best photography in the world, through to powerful image editing apps, capable of handling RAW files, that mean you can edit without your PC. The array of apps currently on the market will blow you away and even more advanced software is being developed right now—make the App Store's photography section something you check on a weekly basis.

This book won't teach you how to take better photos, nor was it intended to, but it will help you to access, edit and share them better. Above all, I hope it has reaffirmed that buying an iPad was a solid investment for you as a photographer, or encouraged you to go out and buy yourself one.

iPad Models

If you don't already own an iPad, hopefully you're ready to make the investment and change the way you work with photos forever, or perhaps you're using an early iPad and are planning an upgrade. Either way, the first question you'll be asking is "Which one do I buy?"

There are three different types of iPad on the market: iPad Mini, iPad 2 and iPad with Retina display. The iPad Mini and iPad with Retina display are available as Wi Fi or Wi Fi plus cellular and the iPad 2 is available as Wi Fi or Wi Fi plus 3G. Then, there are the different sizes: while the iPad 2 comes as 16GB only, the iPad Mini is available as 16GB, 32GB OR 64GB and the iPad with Retina display has the same options, with the addition of a 128GB model.

As with most technology, the more money you spend, the more features you get. In the case of the iPad, the decision is simplified by the nature of the iPad's price-dependent specifications, namely its capacity and Internet connection. If you can do without a web connection wherever you are and won't be frustrated when your devise only holds images from a few photoshoots, then by all means opt for the cheapest model.

Before you make your decision, consider the investment you're making and question whether the added storage constant Internet capacity will be worth your extra money in the long term. If it will, go for the line's top end. Just bear in mind that when you opt for a 3G or Cellular, you have the additional monthly tariff to pay for too, which is comparable to mobile phone service.

Photographer Adam Gasson using his iPad in the studio with the Capture Pilot app.

INDEX

MESSAGES FROM THE PUBLISHER

Keep up to date

Due to the fast-paced nature of technology development and the iPad's ever-increasing array of features, available apps, and updates, some of the information in this book may become out-of-date.

However, we as the publisher want to keep you as current, informed, and up-to-date as possible, and to this end we've dedicated a portion of our website to *iPad for Photographer's* updates. Check www.ilex-press.com/resources/ipad-for-photographers/ for any information regarding new releases.

The Ilex Photo Tool for iPhone

The Ilex Photo Tool for iPhone, iPod touch, and iPad, is a very handy 4-in-1 tool for digital photographers trying to get the best out of the portable camera on their iPhone.

Building on Ilex's heritage as a leading publisher of photography books, the Ilex Photo Tool offers quick and convenient access to everything the photographer needs to get the perfect shot, straight from their pocket.

To learn more and download today, visit the Ilex Photo Tool page on the iTunes Store.

ACKNOWLEDGMENTS

Throughout the writing of this book I have sought the opinions and advice of a wide range of professionals across many disciplines. From photographers to journalists, software developers to web designers, their help has been invaluable and I thank each one of you. Special thanks should go to Corey Rich for refusing to let 10,000 feet and time zones prevent his contributions and to Frederick Van Johnson for putting up with one of the longest email chains I have ever been involved in. Also, thanks should go to the wonderful and understanding Hayley Shore for putting up with the late nights, constant keyboard tapping and my endless out loud thinking.

Ben Harvell 16 June 2011 12:20